TOP **10**
BOSTON

Top 10 Boston Highlights

The Top 10 of Everything

Welcome to Boston **5**

Exploring Boston **6**

Boston Highlights **10**

The Freedom Trail **12**

Museum of Science **16**

Boston Common
    and Public Garden **18**

Harvard University **20**

Around Newbury Street **24**

Museum of Fine Arts, Boston **28**

Trinity Church **32**

Isabella Stewart
    Gardner Museum **34**

Charlestown Navy Yard **36**

New England Aquarium **38**

Moments in History **42**

Figures in Boston's History **44**

Waterfront Areas **46**

Boston Harbor Islands **48**

Off the Beaten Path **50**

Children's Attractions **52**

Performing Arts Venues **54**

Dance and Live
    Music Venues **56**

Gay and Lesbian Hangouts **58**

Bars **60**

Restaurants **62**

Spots for Seafood **64**

Cafés **66**

Essential Shopping
    Experiences **68**

Boston for Free **70**

Festivals and Events **72**

Day Trips:
    Historic New England **74**

Day Trips: The Beach **76**

CONTENTS

Boston Area by Area

Beacon Hill 80

Back Bay 86

North End and
the Waterfront 94

Downtown and the
Financial District 100

Chinatown, the Theater
District, and South End 106

Kenmore and the Fenway 116

Cambridge and Somerville 122

South of Boston 130

Streetsmart

Getting To and Around
Boston 138

Practical Information 140

Places to Stay 146

General Index 152

Acknowledgments 158

Within each Top 10 list in this book, no hierarchy of quality or popularity is implied. All 10 are, in the editor's opinion, of roughly equal merit.
Throughout this book, floors are referred to in accordance with American usage: i.e., the "first floor" is at ground level.

Title page, front cover and spine A stunning view of the Boston skyline from the Charles River
Back cover, clockwise from top left New England Aquarium; Boston Common in winter; Downtown Boston; city skyline; Public Garden

The information in this DK Eyewitness Top 10 Travel Guide is checked regularly. Every effort has been made to ensure that this book is as up-to-date as possible at the time of going to press. Some details, however, such as telephone numbers, opening hours, prices, gallery hanging arrangements and travel information, are liable to change. The publishers cannot accept responsibility for any consequences arising from the use of this book, nor for any material on third-party websites, and cannot guarantee that any website address in this book will be a suitable source of travel information. We value the views and suggestions of our readers very highly. Please write to: Publisher, DK Eyewitness Travel Guides, Dorling Kindersley, 80 Strand, London WC2R 0RL, Great Britain, or email travelguides@dk.com

Welcome to
Boston

City of the future, cradle of American history. Hotbed of innovation, bastion of tradition. Like a polished gem cut from the rocky shores of New England, Boston has so many facets that discovering it can entertain visitors for days on end. It dazzles with renowned museums, great shopping, lush gardens and parks, and vibrant public spaces. With Eyewitness Top 10 Boston, it's yours to explore.

The fastest way to fall in love with Boston is to explore it on foot. Walk the **Freedom Trail** through the heart of Downtown and North End to famous Revolutionary War sites, including the **Paul Revere House**, **Old North Church**, and **Faneuil Hall** You can then explore the vibrant beauty of **Boston Common and Public Garden**, the majesty of **Trinity Church**, and the fun of high-fashion shopping along **Newbury Street**.

When you are ready for a taste of culture, what could be better than an evening listening to the fabled **Boston Symphony Orchestra**, or a visit to the **Museum of Fine Arts, Boston**, or the delightfully eccentric **Isabella Stewart Gardner Museum**? And be sure to explore the remarkable science and art museums of **Harvard University**.

Did we mention the food? With the Atlantic Ocean as its front door and the farms of New England close by, it's no wonder that Boston is renowned for great seafood and farm-to-table-fresh fare, not to mention a wealth of delicious dishes from every part of the world.

Whether you're visiting for a weekend or a week, our Top 10 guide brings together the best of everything the city has to offer, from the historic **Beacon Hill** to the lively **Theater District**. The guide has useful tips throughout, from seeking out what's free to avoiding the crowds, plus 10 easy-to-follow itineraries, designed to tie together a clutch of sights in a short space of time. Add inspiring photography and detailed maps, and you've got the essential pocket-sized travel companion. **Enjoy the book, and enjoy Boston**.

Clockwise from top: **Financial District as seen from Boston Harbor; Federal-style rowhouses in Beacon Hill; Museum of Fine Arts, Boston; a brass marker on the Freedom Trail; Boston Public Garden in fall; buoys in Rockport; Harvard University's Memorial Hall**

Exploring Boston

Whether you have just a couple of days, or more time to explore, there's so much to see and do in Boston. Here are some ideas for how to make the most of your time.

Public Garden is a vibrant green space in the heart of the city.

Two Days in Boston

Day ❶
MORNING

Begin at **Boston Common and Public Garden** (see pp18–19), and pick up a map for the **Freedom Trail** (see pp12–15) at the Information Kiosk. Walk the trail, stopping at **Faneuil Hall** (see p13) for lunch and to shop for souvenirs.

AFTERNOON

Continue along the Freedom Trail to the **Charlestown Navy Yard** (see pp36–7), and then explore the **Museum of Science** (see pp16–17). Pay a visit to **Harvard University** (see pp20–23) for a leisurely walk around campus and then take in a concert at **Sanders Theatre** (see p55).

Day ❷
MORNING

Start off at the **Museum of Fine Arts, Boston** (see pp28–31) and then see the exquisite collections of the **Isabella Stewart Gardner Museum** (see pp34–5). Lunch at **Café G** (see p121).

AFTERNOON

Discover the Romanesque beauty of **Trinity Church** (see pp32–3) before exploring **Newbury Street** (see pp24–5) shopping. In the evening, enjoy a show at the **Boch Center – Wang Theatre** (see p54).

Key

— Two-day itinerary
— Four-day itinerary

Four Days in Boston

Day ❶
MORNING

From **Boston Common and Public Garden** (see pp18–19) explore **Beacon Hill** (see pp80–85) and the antiques shops of **Charles Street** (see p84). Stop for lunch at **Artú** (see p85).

AFTERNOON

Visit the **Isabella Stewart Gardner Museum** (see pp34–5) then dine at **Sorellina** (see p93) before a performance at **Symphony Hall** (see p54).

Day ❷
MORNING

Explore **Back Bay** (see pp86–93), visiting **Trinity Church** (see pp32–3), the **Boston Public Library** (see p87),

Boston waterfront has several attractions, including the Boston Tea Party Ships and Museum.

Trinity Church is famed for its beautiful stained glass.

[Map of central Boston showing locations including Warren Tavern, Charlestown Navy Yard, Museum of Science, Beacon Hill, Charles Street, Public Garden, Newbury Street, Back Bay, Trinity Church, Boston Public Library, Symphony Hall, Faneuil Hall, Artú, Long Wharf, New England Aquarium, Boston Common, Boch Center – Wang Theatre, Boston Tea Party Ships and Museum, Legal Harborside, orellina]

0 meters 750
0 yards 750

and the art galleries and shops that make **Newbury Street** *(see p91)* a shopper's paradise.

AFTERNOON
Spend the afternoon at the Museum of Fine Arts, Boston *(see pp20–31)*, followed by a waterside seafood dinner at **Legal Harborside** *(see p64)*.

Day ❸
MORNING
Walk the **Freedom Trail** *(see pp12–15)*, pausing at **Faneuil Hall** *(see p13)* for coffee and a snack. At the end of the trail, tour the **Charlestown Navy Yard** *(see pp36–7)* and stop for lunch at the historic **Warren Tavern** *(see p37)*.

AFTERNOON
Head over to the **New England Aquarium** *(see pp38–9)* and marvel at the marine life on display. Then take in the nearby **Boston Tea Party Ships**

and Museum *(see p96)*, joining in with the revolutionary fun. Complete the day on a **Boston Harbor Cruise** *(see p139)*, departing from **Long Wharf** *(see p46)*.

Day ❹
MORNING
Start at the **John F. Kennedy Library and Museum** *(see p133)* before exploring the campus at JFK's alma mater, **Harvard University** *(see pp20–23)*.

AFTERNOON
After lunch in **Harvard Square** and a browse around its bookstores *(see p69)* visit the **Peabody and Natural History Museums** *(see p123)* and then head over to the fascinating **Museum of Science** *(see p52)*. If the Red Sox are playing an evening game, head over to **Fenway Park** *(see p117)*, but if you can't get hold of tickets, just make your way to **Game On!** *(see p120)*, the on-site sports bar, and watch a live broadcast of the game there.

Top 10 Boston Highlights

**Courtyard of the Isabella
Stewart Gardner Museum**

Boston Highlights	10	Trinity Church	32
The Freedom Trail	12	Isabella Stewart Gardner Museum	34
Museum of Science	16	Charlestown Navy Yard	36
Boston Common and Public Garden	18	New England Aquarium	38
Harvard University	20		
Around Newbury Street	24		
Museum of Fine Arts, Boston	28		

📱10 Boston Highlights

With its colonial-era architecture, lively seafaring heritage, and irrepressible Yankee character, Boston is one of the country's most distinctive locales. And, for all its big-city amenities – world-class restaurants, museums, and stores – visitors find it delightfully compact and walkable.

The Freedom Trail ①

Boston's best walking tour is free, full of history, and open year round (see pp12–15). It passes various sights, including the Paul Revere House (see p95) where items such as colonial banknotes can be seen.

② Museum of Science

One of Boston's liveliest and most-visited science museums, this remarkable facility delights with over 700 fascinating inter-active exhibits (see pp16–17).

③ Boston Common and Public Garden

Swan boats drift beneath weeping willows, children splash in fountains, and a bronzed George Washington oversees the proceed-ings from his lofty steed (see pp18–19).

④ Harvard University

Established in 1636, the undisputed heart of American academia has cultivated some of the world's greatest thinkers and statesmen, including eight US pres-idents (see pp20–23).

⑤ Around Newbury Street
Where fashionistas share the sidewalk with punk rockers. Nowhere are the city's myriad fashions, faces, and fortunes on more vibrant display *(see pp24–5)*.

⑥ Museum of Fine Arts, Boston
Boston's queen of the visual arts scene boasts one of the most extensive collections of Japanese, ancient Egyptian, and Impressionist works of art in the Americas *(see pp28–31)*.

⑦ Trinity Church
This Romanesque Revival church is considered the finest work by architect H. H. Richardson. Equally impressive is La Farge's *Christ in Majesty* window *(see pp32–3)*.

⑧ Isabella Stewart Gardner Museum
Masterpieces by the likes of Rembrandt, Botticelli, and Raphael appear all the more magnificent set in Isabella Stewart Gardner's Venetian-style palazzo built around a leafy courtyard *(see pp34–5)*.

⑨ Charlestown Navy Yard
Boston's deep harbor was ideal for one of the US Navy's first shipyards. The USS *Constitution*, built in 1797 (3 years prior to the Yard), is still docked here *(see pp36–7)*.

⑩ New England Aquarium
Get up close to three species of penguins, playful harbor seals, and myriad other creatures of the deep *(see pp38–9)*.

★ The Freedom Trail

Snaking through 2.5 miles (4 km) of city streets, the Freedom Trail is a living link to Boston's key revolutionary and colonial-era sites. As you walk it, you'll see history adopt a vibrancy and palpability unparalleled among US cities. Some of Boston's most special stores, restaurants, and attractions are also located along the Trail.

1 Massachusetts State House

Boston architect Charles Bulfinch's *pièce de résistance*, the "new" State House (completed in 1798) is one of the city's most distinctive buildings *(see p81)*.

6 Old State House

Built in 1713, this handsome colonial building **(left)** was the headquarters of the colonial legislature and the Royal Governor. The Declaration of Independence was first read from its balcony *(see p101)*.

4 King's Chapel

The current granite building dates from around 1749, although the chapel was originally founded in 1686 by King James II as an outpost of the Anglican Church *(see p103)*. Don't miss the burying ground next door, which shelters Massachusetts' first Governor, John Winthrop *(see p44)*.

2 Park Street Church

Founded by a small group of Christians disenchanted with their Unitarian-leaning congregation, Park Street Church **(above)** was dedicated in 1810.

5 Old South Meeting House

Boston's Old South Meeting House *(see p102)* was, to the colonial era, a crucible for free-speech debates and protests against taxation.

3 Old Granary Burying Ground

A veritable who's-who of revolutionary history fertilizes this plot **(right)** next to Park Street Church *(see p101)*. One of its most venerable residents is Samuel Adams *(see p44)*.

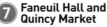

7 Faneuil Hall and Quincy Market

Known as the "Cradle of Liberty," Faneuil Hall has played host to many a revolutionary meeting in its time. Neighboring Quincy Market **(below)**, built in the early 1800s, once housed Boston's wholesale food distribution *(see p101)*.

AN HOUR OF FREEDOM

For visitors tight on time, consider this condensed trail. Head up Tremont Street from Park Street "T" station, stopping to visit the Old Granary Burying Ground. At the corner of Tremont and School streets – site of King's Chapel – turn right onto School and continue to Washington Street and the Old South Meeting House. Turn left on Washington to the Old State House then finish up at Faneuil Hall nearby on Congress Street.

8 Paul Revere House

In North Square, the Paul Revere House *(see p95)* is Boston's oldest private residence. Its principal owner *(see p44)* was well regarded locally as a metalsmith prior to his history-changing ride.

9 Old North Church

This church **(below)** has a pivotal place in revolutionary history *(see p95)*. Prior to his midnight ride, Revere *(see p44)* ordered Robert Newman to hang one or two lamps in the belfry to indicate, respectively, whether the British were approaching by land or via the Charles River.

NEED TO KNOW

MAP P4 ■ Start point: Boston Common. "T" station: Park St (red/green lines) ■ Finish point: Charlestown. "T" station: Community College (orange line) ■ www.thefreedom trail.org

Park Street Church: 1 Park St; 617 523 3383; www.parkstreet.org

■ Give your sweet tooth a workout at Mike's Pastry *(see p98)*.

■ Maps of the trail are available at the Boston Common Visitor Center, or at the Boston National Park headquarters at Faneuil Hall, where free, ranger-led walking tours are offered by the National Park Service.

■ Most of the trail is indicated in red paint with a few sections in red brick.

10 Copp's Hill Burying Ground

With headstones dating from the 17th century, Copp's Hill *(see p95)* is a must for history buffs. It was named after William Copp, a farmer who sold the land to the church.

Moments in Revolutionary History

The Battle of Lexington

1 **Resistance to the Stamp Act (1765)**

The king imposed a stamp duty on all published materials in the colonies, including newspapers. Furious Bostonians boycotted British goods in response.

2 **Boston Massacre (1770)**

Angry colonists picked a fight with British troops in front of the Old State House, resulting in the deaths of five unarmed Bostonians.

3 **Samuel Adams' Tea Tax Speech (1773)**

Adams' incendiary speech during a forum at the Old South Meeting House inspired the Boston Tea Party, the most subversive action undertaken yet in the debate over colonial secession.

4 **Boston Tea Party (1773)**

Led by Samuel Adams, the Sons of Liberty boarded three British East India Company ships and dumped their cargo into the Boston Harbor, a watershed moment of colonial defiance.

Bust of George Washington, Old North Church

5 **Paul Revere's Ride (1775)**

Revere rode to Lexington to warn revolutionaries Samuel Adams and John Hancock that British troops intended to arrest them. One of the bravest acts of the war, it would be immortalized in the Longfellow poem *The Midnight Ride of Paul Revere*.

6 **Battle of Lexington (1775)**

Revere's ride was followed by the first exchange of fire between the ragtag colonist army and the British at Lexington.

7 **Battle of Bunker Hill (1775)**

The colonists' fortification of Charlestown resulted in a full-scale British attack. Despite their defeat, the colonists' resolve was galvanized by this battle.

8 **Washington Takes Command (1776)**

The Virginia gentleman farmer George Washington led the newly formed Continental Army south from Cambridge to face British troops in New York.

9 **Fortification of Dorchester Heights (1776)**

Fortifying the mouth of Boston Harbor with captured cannon, George Washington put the Royal Navy under his guns and forced a British retreat from the city.

10 **Declaration of Independence (1776)**

On July 4, the colonies rejected all allegiance to the British Crown. In Boston, Independence was declared from the Royal Governor's head-quarters, the building known today as the Old State House (see p12).

MASSACHUSETTS STATE HOUSE

Finished in 1798, the State House is Charles Bulfinch's masterwork. With its brash design details, imposing stature, and liberal use of fine materials, it embodies the optimism of post-revolutionary America. The building is in three distinct sections: the original Bulfinch front; the marble wings constructed in 1917; and the yellow-brick 1895 addition, known as the Brigham Extension after the architect who designed it. Just below Bulfinch's central colonnade, statues of famous Massachusetts figures strike poses. Among them are the great orator Daniel Webster; President John F. Kennedy; and Quaker Mary Dyer, who was hanged in 1660 for challenging the authority of Boston's religious leaders. Directly below the State House's immense gilded dome is the Senate Chamber, site of many influential speeches and debates. After an extensive renovation, the historic chamber reopened in early 2019.

TOP 10
STATE HOUSE FEATURES

1 23-carat gold dome

2 Senate Chamber

3 House of Representatives

4 "Hear Us" exhibit

5 Stained-glass windows

6 Doric Hall

7 Hall of Flags

8 Nurses Hall

9 Sacred Cod

10 State House Pine Cone

The Sacred Cod was bestowed on the House of Representatives by Boston merchant Jonathan Rowe. This carved fish has presided over the Commonwealth's legislature since 1784, though it vanished briefly in 1933, when Harvard's *Lampoon* magazine orchestrated a dastardly "codnapping" prank.

Facade of the Massachusetts State House

🏆10 ⭐ Museum of Science

With over 700 colorful, interactive displays designed to thrill and amaze the minds of kids and adults alike, it's little wonder that this is one of Boston's most-visited museums. Popular attractions include the jaw-dropping dome-shaped IMAX® screen in the Mugar Omni Theater, the techno-fabulous Hall of Human Life, kid-pleasing lightning demonstrations, and daily live science shows.

5 Hall of Human Life

Visitors here are given an anonymous barcode wristband that is used to record their responses to the many challenges and activities on offer, and can then download their results and compare them to those of other visitors. Cutting-edge subjects are explored, such as DNA sequencing, GMO research and all sorts of medical and nutritional issues **(left)**.

1 To the Moon

This popular exhibit includes full-size replicas of the Apollo Command Module and the Lunar Module cockpit. Kids can climb into the pilots' seats and relive the first landing on the moon. Nearby models show the growth of space stations from Skylab and Mir to the International Space Station. Pieces of moon rock are on show as well.

2 Butterfly Garden

Visitors to this tropical greenhouse walk among clouds of brightly colored, fluttering butterflies from New England and around the world. Interactive displays and exhibits highlight fascinating butterfly facts including the four stages of a butterfly's life, plus the miracle of metamorphosis, and how they fly.

3 Colossal Fossil

Meet Cliff, one of only four nearly complete triceratops skeletons on display in the world. He looks pretty good considering he's 65 million years old. Discovered in North Dakota in 2004, Cliff measures 23 ft (7 m) from horn tip to tail, and his head alone weighs 800 lb (362 kg).

4 Discovery Center

Geared to children under eight, this colorful, fun, activity-filled center is all about stimulating young minds with a sense of exploration. The changing activities can include excavating artifacts, analyzing fingerprints, or creating slime with borax and school glue. Well-trained staff help children discover the fun of problem-solving.

6 Theater of Electricity

This live-theater show explores the science of electricity. Its star is the world's largest Van de Graaff generator **(above)**, which safely zaps out sizzling lightning bolts of up to 1 million volts.

7 Charles Hayden Planetarium

This high-tech planetarium brings the dazzling night sky to life, and presents shows that include a look at images sent back by NASA's latest space missions, exploration of celestial sights, and immersive music shows.

Key to Floor Plan
- Second floor
- First floor
- Lower floor

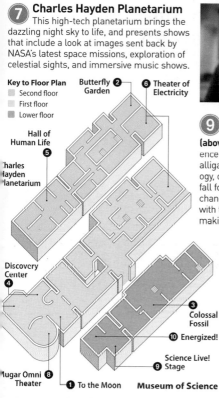

Butterfly Garden **2**

6 Theater of Electricity

Hall of Human Life **5**

Charles Hayden Planetarium

Discovery Center **4**

Mugar Omni **8** Theater

1 To the Moon

3 Colossal Fossil

10 Energized!

Science Live! **9** Stage

Museum of Science

9 Science Live! Stage

This live presentation (above) features hands-on science demonstrations. Meet an alligator, explore nanotechnology, or find out why our brains fall for optical illusions. A daily changing schedule keeps up with the latest advancements making the news.

10 Energized!

Innovative exhibits cover the latest in alternative energy, including solar, wind, and hydroelectric power, and the solutions they can offer.

MUSEUM HISTORY

The Boston Museum of Science traces its origins back to the founding of the Boston Society of Natural History in 1830. The first permanent museum opened in 1864, making MOS one of the oldest science museums in America.

8 Mugar Omni Theater

This remarkable IMAX® Theater takes the "big-screen" concept into a whole new realm. Visitors sit below a 180-degree dome that fills their entire range of vision, immersing their senses with spectacular sights and powerful digital sounds.

NEED TO KNOW

MAP G3 ▪ 1 Science Park ▪ "T" station: Science Park (green line) ▪ 617 723 2500 ▪ www.mos.org

Open 9am–5pm Sat–Thu (Jul & Aug: to 7pm), 9am–9pm Fri

Adm adults $28; seniors $24; children (aged 3–11) $23

An extra fee is charged for admission to several attractions, including the Charles Hayden Planetarium, the 4-D Theater, the Mugar Omni Theater and the Butterfly Garden. Individual admission to these attractions ranges from $6 to $10.

▪ The museum's Riverview Café (level 1, by the Museum Store)

features several food stations, including a taqueria, Puck's (light meals designed by celebrity chef Wolfgang Puck), a burger grill, salad bar, sandwich stand, and a Starbucks coffee shop. Special meal options are available for large groups that call ahead and make a booking to visit the Museum of Science.

🔟⭐ Boston Common and Public Garden

Verdant Boston Common has hosted auctions, cattle grazing, and public hangings over its 380-year history, in addition to festivals and the requisite frisbee tosses. The adjacent Public Garden, opened in 1839, was the US's first botanical garden. Its swan boats and weeping willows are emblematic of Boston at its most enchanting. The French-style flowerbeds may only bloom in warmer months, but the garden exudes old-world charm year round.

1 Frog Pond
During summer, children splash under the iridescent spray of the pond's fountains **(above)**. Come winter, kids of all ages lace up their skates and take to the ice. Skate rentals and delicious hot chocolate are nearby.

2 Lagoon Bridge
This elegant 1869 faux suspension bridge crossing the lagoon has served as the romantic setting for many wedding photos.

3 Make Way for Ducklings Statuettes
Eight little ducklings seem to have sprung from the pages of Robert McCloskey's much-loved kids' book and fallen in line behind their mother at the lagoon's edge **(right)**.

4 Shaw Memorial
Augustus Saint-Gaudens' lifelike bronze pays homage to the "Fighting 54th" – one of the only entirely African-American regiments in the Civil War. Led by Boston native Robert Shaw, the 54th amassed an impressive battle record.

5 Bronze of George Washington
The nation's first president cuts a stately figure at the western end of the Public Garden **(above)**. Local sculptor Thomas Ball's 1869 bronze was an early horseback depiction of Washington.

6 Soldiers and Sailors Monument
Over 25,000 Union Army veterans remembered their fallen Civil War comrades at the 1877 dedication of Martin Milmore's impressive memorial. Bas-reliefs depict the soldiers' and sailors' departure to and return from war.

Map of Boston Common and Public Garden

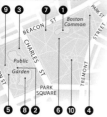

7 Founders' Memorial

William Blaxton, Boston's first white settler, is depicted greeting John Winthrop *(see p44)* in John F. Paramino's 1930 bronze. Note the use of the word "Shawmut" – the Native American name for the land that would become Boston.

8 Swan Boats

Summer hasn't officially arrived in Boston until the swan boats emerge from hibernation and glide onto the Public Garden lagoon. With their gracefully arching necks and brilliantly painted bills, each distinctive swan can accommodate up to 20 people.

10 Parkman Bandstand

Built in 1912 to honor George Parkman, a benefactor of the park, this elegant bandstand **(left)** is modeled on Versailles' *Temple d'Amour* (temple of love). It hosts everything from concerts to political rallies.

9 Ether Monument

This 1868 statue commemorates the first etherized operation, which took place at Massachusetts General Hospital in 1846 *(see p51)*. Controversial from the outset, this is the West's only monument to the powers of a drug.

EMERALD NECKLACE

Boston Common and Public Garden may seem like solitary urban oases, but they are two links in a greater chain of green space that stretches all the way through Boston to the suburb of Roxbury. The Emerald Necklace, as this chain is called, was completed in 1896 by Frederick Law Olmsted, the man behind New York's Central Park.

NEED TO KNOW

MAP M4, N4

■ Bounded by: Beacon, Park, Tremont, Arlington, & Boylston streets

■ "T" station: Park Street (red/green line), Boylston & Arlington (both green line)

Boston Common Visitor Center: 139 Tremont St; 617 426 3115; open 8:30am–5pm Mon–Fri, 9am–5pm Sat & Sun (shorter weekend hours in winter)

Boston Parks & Recreation: 617 635 4505; www.cityof boston.gov/parks

Swan Boat Rides: 617 522 1966; open mid-Apr–mid-Sep: 10am–5pm daily; adm $4; www.swanboats.com

■ Quick, food-court-style bites can be had inside the Corner shopping center at Washington and Summer streets.

■ The Commonwealth Shakespeare Company *(see p71)* stages free performances during summer.

TOP 10 ⭐ Harvard University

America's most prestigious university – founded in 1636 and named for its earliest benefactor, John Harvard, in 1638 – has nurtured, tortured, and tickled some of the greatest minds of the past 380 years. It has hosted everything from global economic summits to psyche-delic drug experiments, and educated future US presidents to talk-show hosts. Visitors craving contact with the Harvard mys-tique are in luck – much of the university is open to the public.

1 Massachusetts Hall

The university's oldest building, constructed in 1720, was once a barrack for 640 revo-lutionary soldiers. The hall houses the office of the President of Harvard and is usually the centre of protests against university policies.

2 John Harvard Statue

The inscription "John Harvard, Founder 1638" conceals three deceptions, hence its nickname "The Statue of Three Lies." First, there is no known portrait of John Harvard, so the sculptor used a model; second, Harvard did not found the university – it was named after him; and last, it was founded in 1636, not 1638.

3 Memorial Hall

Built over 8 years, Harvard's memorial to its fallen Union army alumni was officially opened in 1878. Con-ceived as a multipurpose building, it has hosted graduation exercises, theatrical performances, and assemblies of many other kinds **(above)**.

5 Harvard Yard

Harvard's mixed residential and academic yard became the stan-dard by which most American institutions of higher learning modeled their campuses.

6 Harry Widener Memorial Library

The Widener is the largest university library in the US. It houses an extremely impressive collection of rare books, including a Gutenberg Bible and early editions of Shakespeare's collected works.

4 Museum of Natural History

The exhibits at this museum [see p123] include George Washington's taxidermied pheasants, the Brazilian amethyst geode, the mounted Kronosaurus skeleton, and glass flowers – 850 species of plants, painstakingly replicated in colorful glass **(above)**.

Flagstaff Park

PEABODY ST

CHURCH ST

Old Yard

HARVARD SQUARE

Harvard

DUNSTER ST

MASSACHUS

HOLYOKE ST

Map of Harvard University

9 Harvard Art Museums

Harvard's three art museums *(see p123)* were brought under one roof in a Renzo Piano building in 2014. It displays works **(above)** from Fogg Museum's world-class collection of European and American art, Germanic art holdings of the Busch-Reisinger Museum, and Asian collections of the Sackler Museum.

10 Science Center Plaza

This plaza in front of the Undergraduate Science Center is Harvard's busiest social space, featuring the Tanner Fountain, benches, and food trucks.

7 Semitic Museum

Founded in 1889, this museum houses more than 40,000 objects from excavations in Egypt, Iraq, Israel, Jordan, Syria, and Tunisia.

8 Peabody Museum

One of the world's most comprehensive records of human cultural history, the Peabody *(see p123)* caters for the Indiana Jones in all of us. Highlights include Encounters with the Americas **(below)**, a permanent Mesoamerica exhibit, and a gallery devoted to the development of the science of archaeology.

HARVARD LAMPOON

Lampooners have made you laugh more than you might ever know. Aside from *The Harvard Lampoon* being the world's oldest humor magazine, nearly every successful contemporary American comedy to reach a television or movie screen boasts an ex-Lampooner on its writing staff. Well-known ex-Lampooners include the popular late-night TV host Conan O'Brien.

NEED TO KNOW

MAP B1–C1 ■ "T" station: Harvard (red line) ■ www.harvard. edu; www.cambridge usa.org

Harry Widener Memorial Library: Harvard Yard; 617 495 2413; book tour 2–3pm Fri; access only if accompanied by someone with valid Harvard ID

Semitic Museum: 6 Divinity Ave; 617 495 4631; open 11am–4pm Sun–Fri

Maps and campus tours available from Smith Campus Center: 1350 Massachusetts Ave; 617 495 1573

■ Students refuel at the Harvard Coop bookstore café (1400 Massachusetts Ave, 617 499 2000).

■ Harvard Film Archive, Carpenter Center, screens art and documentary films most nights (24 Quincy St, 617 495 4700).

Harvard Alumni

1 John Adams (1735–1826)
The nation's second president, although nervous upon entering the illustrious college as a freshman, eventually became enthralled by his studies.

2 Henry James (1843–1916)
The master of the psychological novel sourced plenty of material at Harvard for his scathing 1886 work *The Bostonians*.

3 W. E. B. Du Bois (1868–1963)
Founder of the National Association for the Advancement of Colored People (NAACP), Du Bois studied philosophy here, and said of his experience, "I was in Harvard, but not of it."

4 Franklin Delano Roosevelt (1882–1945)
Apparently more of a social butterfly than a dedicated academic, F.D.R. played pranks, led the freshman football squad, edited the *Harvard Crimson*, and earned a C average at Harvard before going on to become the 32nd President of the US.

5 T. S. Eliot (1885–1965)
The modernist poet of *The Waste Land* fame contributed much of his early work to the *Advocate*. He went on to edit many of those submissions for later publication.

6 John F. Kennedy (1917–63)
A barely average student, but a good athlete, John F. Kennedy ran for President of the Freshman Class in 1936, and lost badly. He did rather better in 1960 when he became the 35th President of the United States.

Leonard Bernstein

7 Leonard Bernstein (1918–90)
The country's greatest composer and conductor was firmly grounded in the arts at Harvard. He edited the *Advocate* – the college's estimable literary and performing arts journal.

8 Benazir Bhutto (1953–2007)
This class of 1973 alumna later became the first woman to lead a modern Muslim state when she was elected prime minister of Pakistan in 1988. She was assassinated in 2007.

9 Bill Gates (1955–)
William Henry Gates III dropped out of Harvard in his third year to found Microsoft. He was made an Honorary Knight Commander of the Order of the British Empire (KBE) by Queen Elizabeth II in 2005 for his humanitarian and philanthropic work. He was also awarded an honorary doctorate in 2007 by Harvard.

Bill Gates

10 Barack Obama (1961–)
The 44th President of the United States attended Harvard Law School from 1988–91. His election as the first black president of the *Harvard Law Review* gained extensive media attention.

HARVARD'S "ARCHITECTURAL ZOO"

Prominent modernist architect James Stirling described Harvard as an "architectural zoo" – and it's a well-deserved moniker. Stirling was responsible for the university's modernist 1985 Sackler Museum building *(see p123)* that now houses offices. Charles Bulfinch, whose claim to fame is the Massachusetts State House *(see p12),* contributed the 1814 University Hall, featuring an ingenious granite staircase that "floats" – supported solely by virtue of its interlocking steps. In contrast, Walter Gropius, whose strongly linear residential buildings pepper college campuses throughout the northeast US, designed the Harvard Graduate Center in 1950. He strove to make his industry-informed projects seem welcoming for their inhabitants, but by most Harvard grad students' accounts, it doesn't exactly scream "home sweet home." Le Corbusier's Carpenter Center for the Visual Arts is a wondrous collection of forms and materials. The center boasts entire walls made of glass and deeply grooved concrete. Perhaps surprisingly, it is Le Corbusier's only design in North America.

Sever Hall and Austin Hall were designed by architect and 1859 Harvard alumnus H. H. Richardson. Both halls echo the distinctive Romanesque style found on his Copley Square masterpiece – Trinity Church *(see pp32–3).*

TOP 10
HARVARD'S BUILDINGS

1 Memorial Hall, 45 Quincy St (Ware and Van Brunt, 1878)

2 Loeb Drama Center, 64 Brattle St (Hugh Stebbins, 1959)

3 Massachusetts Hall, Harvard Yard (University Overseers, 1720)

4 Sackler Museum building, 485 Broadway (James Stirling, 1985)

5 Harvard Art Museums, 32 Quincy Street (Renzo Piano and Payette, 2014)

6 University Hall, Harvard Yard (Charles Bulfinch, 1814)

7 Sever and Austin halls, Harvard Yard and North Yard (H. H. Richardson, 1880 and 1883)

8 Harvard Graduate Center, North Yard (Walter Gropius, 1950)

9 Carpenter Center for the Visual Arts, 24 Quincy St (Le Corbusier, 1963)

10 Undergraduate Science Center, Oxford St (Josep Lluís Sert, 1971)

Carpenter Center for Visual Arts, designed by Le Corbusier

🔟 ⭐ Around Newbury Street

Don't let the profusion of Prada-clad shoppers fool you: there's much more to elegant Newbury Street than world-class retail, people-watching, and alfresco dining. One of the first streets created on the marshland once known as Back Bay, Newbury has seen myriad tenants and uses over the past 150 years. Look closely and you'll glimpse a historical side to Newbury Street all but unseen by the fashionistas.

3 Church of the Covenant

English-born architect Richard Upjohn left his Neo-Gothic mark on Boston with the Church of the Covenant (left), erected in 1865. It has the world's largest collection of Tiffany stained glass.

4 Kingsley Montessori School

Built as a Spiritualist temple in 1884, this building became the dignified Exeter Street Theater in 1914. In 2005, it was converted to a private school.

1 Emmanuel Church

Architect Alexander Estey's impressive church (1860) was the first building to grace Newbury after the infilling of Back Bay. The adjacent Lindsey Chapel (1924) is home to the renowned Emmanuel Music ensemble.

5 New England Historic Genealogical Society

Members seek to discover more about their New England progenitors in one of the most extensive genealogical libraries in the US.

2 French Cultural Center

Housed in a grand Back Bay mansion, the French Cultural Center hosts everything from lectures in French to concerts and a tasteful Bastille Day celebration. It also runs year-round courses in French for all ages.

6 234 Berkeley St

Originally a natural history museum opened in 1864, this landmark building is now a high-end home goods store.

7 Commonwealth Avenue

A mall running along the center of Commonwealth Avenue provides a leafy respite from the Newbury Street throngs. Benches and historical sculptures (left), line the pedestrian path (see p88).

9 Gibson House Museum

One of Back Bay's first private homes, Gibson House **(left)** was also one of the most modern residences of its day. With its gas lighting, indoor plumbing, and heating, it spurred a building boom in the area *(see p88)*.

BACK BAY'S ORIGINS

Since its settlement by Europeans, Boston has been reshaped to suit the needs of its inhabitants. Back Bay derives its name from the tidal swampland on which the neighborhood now stands. During the 19th century, gravel was used to fill the marsh and create the foundations for the grand avenues and picturesque brownstone buildings that now distinguish this sought-after area.

10 Boston Architectural College

For more than 125 years, aspiring architects have studied at this college **(below)**. The McCormick Gallery hosts a number of changing exhibitions.

Shops on Newbury Street

8 Trinity Church Rectory

H. H. Richardson, Trinity Church's principal architect, was commissioned to build this rectory in 1879. His handiwork echoes the Romanesque style of the church itself on Copley Square *(see pp32–3)*.

NEED TO KNOW

MAP K5, L5, M5

■ "T" station: Arlington, Copley, or Hynes/ICA

Boston Architectural College: 320 Newbury St; 617 585 0100; open 8am–10:30pm Mon–Thu, 8am–8pm Fri–Sun

Church of the Covenant: 67 Newbury St

Emmanuel Church: 15 Newbury St

French Cultural Center: 53 Marlborough St; 617 912 0400; open 9am–9pm Mon–Thu, 9am–5pm Fri; longer hours in summer

New England Historic Genealogical Society: 101 Newbury St; 617 536 5740; open 9am–5pm Tue–Sat (until 9pm Wed)

Kingsley Montessori School: 26 Exeter St; not open to the public

Trinity Church Rectory: 233 Clarendon St; not open to the public

....

■ Buy picnic supplies at Deluca's Back Bay Market (239 Newbury St).

■ View the schedule for Emmanuel Music at www.emmanuelmusic.org

Following pages Aerial view of Boston Harbor

TOP 10 ⭐ Museum of Fine Arts, Boston

Over its 140-year-plus history, the MFA has collected around 500,000 pieces from an array of cultures and civilizations, ranging from ancient Egyptian tomb treasures to stylish modern artworks. In 2010, the museum opened its long-anticipated Art of the Americas wing, designed by Norman Foster, which displays works created in North, Central, and South America.

4 Sargent Murals

Having secured some of John Singer Sargent's most important portraiture in the early 20th century, the MFA went one step further and commissioned the artist to paint murals and bas-reliefs on its central rotunda and colonnade. They feature gods and heroes from classical mythology.

1 The Fog Warning

This late 19th-century painting by Winslow Homer is part of a series in which the artist depicted the difficult lives of the local fishermen and their families.

3 Egyptian Royal Pectoral

This extremely rare chest ornament **(above)** is nearly 4,000 years old. A vulture is depicted with a cobra on its left wing, poised to strike.

5 Dance at Bougival

This endearing image (1883) of a young couple dancing is one of the most beloved of Renoir's works. It exemplifies the artist's knack for taking a timeless situation and making it contemporary by dressing his subjects in the latest fashions.

6 Silverwork by Paul Revere

Famed for his midnight ride, Revere *(see p44)* was also known for his masterful silverwork **(left)**. The breadth of his ability is apparent in the museum's magnificent 200-piece collection.

2 John Singleton Copley Portraits

Self-taught, Boston-born Copley made a name for himself by painting the most affluent and influential Bostonians of his day **(right)**, from pre-revolutionary figures like John Hancock to early American presidents such as John Adams.

8 La Japonaise
Claude Monet's 1876 portrait **(left)** reflects a time when Japanese culture fascinated Europe's most style-conscious circles. The model, interestingly, is Monet's wife, Camille.

9 Japanese Temple Room
With its wood paneling and subdued lighting, the Temple Room evokes ancient Japanese shrines atop mist-enshrouded mountains. The statues, which date from as early as the 7th century, depict prominent figures from Buddhist texts.

10 Statue of King Aspelta
This statue **(right)** of the 6th-century BC Nubian king, Aspelta, was recovered in 1920 at Nuri in present-day Sudan during a Museum of Fine Arts/ Harvard joint expedition.

7 Christ in Majesty with Symbols
Acquired in 1919 from a small Spanish church, this medieval fresco had an amazingly complex journey to Boston, which involved waterproofing it with lime and Parmesan for safe transportation.

NEED TO KNOW

MAP D6 ▪ 465 Huntington Ave (Ave of the Arts) ▪ 617 267 9300 ▪ www.mfa.org ▪ "T" station: Museum (green line/E train)

Open 10am–5pm Sat–Tue, 10am–10pm Wed–Fri

Adm $23–$25

▪ The MFA has four restaurants and cafés, which escalate in quality and price as you move from the courtyard level upward. Ideal for a post-gallery drink.

▪ On weekends, the MFA's Family Art Cart in the Shapiro Family Courtyard provides activities and materials to use in the galleries. Consult the museum's website for a full schedule of events.

▪ Admission to the museum on Wednesdays 4–9:45pm is by voluntary donation.

Gallery Guide
European, Classical, Far Eastern, and Egyptian art and artifacts occupy the original MFA building.

The informative Visitor Center is located on Level 1. The Linde Wing for Contemporary Art, on the west side of the museum, also houses the museum shop, cafés, and a restaurant. Arts from the Americas are spread across four levels in the Art of the Americas wing, on the east side of the museum. The wing has 49 galleries, plus a state-of-the-art auditorium, and displays over 5,000 works of art.

Museum of Fine Arts Collections

1 Art of Asia

For Asian art connoisseurs, the museum offers a dizzying overview of Japan's multiple artistic forms. In fact, the MFA holds the largest collection of ancient Japanese art outside of Japan. In addition to the tranquil Temple Room *(see p29)*, with its centuries-old Buddhist statues, visitors should look out for the beautiful hanging scrolls and woodblock prints, with their magical, dramatic landscapes and spirited renderings of everyday life. Kurasawa fans, meanwhile, will be enthralled by the menacing samurai weaponry. Additionally, the Art of Asia collection contains exquisite objects from 2,000 years of Chinese, Indian, and Southeast Asian history, including sensuous ivory figurines, pictorial carpets, and vibrant watercolors.

Stuart woman's doublet, dated from 1610–15

Japan "Golden Age" (1781–1801) print

2 Textile and Fashion Arts

Rotating displays highlight pictorial quilts, period fashions, fine Persian rugs, and pre-colonial Andean weavings. Particularly interesting are the textiles and costumes from the Elizabethan and Stuart periods – an unprecedented 1943 donation from the private collection of Elizabeth Day McCormick.

3 Classical Art

The remarkable Classical Art Collection has a hoard of gold bracelets, glass, mosaic bowls, and stately marble busts. One of the earliest pieces is a c.1500 BC gold axe, inscribed with symbols from a still-undeciphered Cretan language.

4 Art of the Americas

The MFA's Art of the Americas wing, designed by Norman Foster, opened in 2010. The wing features pieces dating from pre-Columbian times, through to the third quarter of the 20th century, and showcases about 5,000 works produced in North, Central, and South America. The museum has profited from generous benefactors over the years and the collection holds the world's finest ensemble of colonial New England furniture, rare 17th-century American portraiture, a superb display of American silver, and paintings by the country's own "Old" Masters, including Copley, Stuart, Cole, Sargent, Cassat, Homer, and many others.

5 Art of Egypt, Nubia, and the Ancient Near East

This collection is a treasure trove of millennia-old Egyptian sarcophagi, tomb finds, and Nubian jewelry and

Egyptian mummy mask (AD 1–50)

objects from everyday life. The assemblage of Egyptian funerary pieces, including beautifully crafted jewelry and ceramic urns, is quite awe-inspiring. Ancient Near Eastern objects, with their bold iconography and rich materials, illustrate why the region is known as the Cradle of Civilization.

6 European Art to 1900

From 12th-century tempera baptism paintings to Claude Monet's *Haystacks*, the MFA's European collection is staggeringly diverse. Painstakingly transferred medieval stained-glass windows, beautifully illuminated bibles, and delicate French tapestries are displayed alongside works by Old Masters: Titian, El Greco, Rembrandt, and Rubens. A superlative Impressionist and Post-Impressionist collection boasts masterpieces from the likes of Renoir, Degas, Cézanne, and Van Gogh, plus the finest group of Monet's works outside of Paris.

La Berceuse (1889) by Van Gogh

7 Contemporary Art

Given Boston's affinity for the traditional, you might be surprised by this world-class collection of contemporary and late 20th-century art. It includes works by the painter and photographer Chuck Close and the Abstract Expressionist artist Jackson Pollock, which are on display in the Art of the Americas wing. New Media is also well represented here.

Tibetan conch shell trumpet

8 Musical Instruments

Priceless 17th-century guitars, ornately inlaid pianos, and even a mouth organ are on view to visitors of the MFA. Among the more distinctive pieces is a c.1796 English grand piano – the earliest extant example of a piano with a six-octave range – and a 1680 French guitar by the Voboam workshop.

9 Art of Africa and Oceania

Pre-colonial artifacts from these collections include Melanese canoe ornaments, dramatic Congolese bird sculptures and African funerary art. The most popular African display is the powerful-looking 19th- and 20th-century wooden masks.

10 "Please be Seated!" Installations

View (and sit on) one of the country's most comprehensive collections of American contemporary furniture. The museum encourages visitors to admire and sit on these furniture pieces. Take a break and have a seat on fine American handiwork by designers such as Maloof, Castle, and Eames.

TOP 10 ⭐ Trinity Church

Boston has a great knack for creating curious visual juxtapositions, and one of the most remarkable is in Copley Square, where Henry Hobson Richardson's 19th-century Romanesque Revival Trinity Church reflects in the sleek, blue-tinted glass of the decidedly 20th-century 200 Clarendon Tower nearby. The breathtakingly beautiful church was named a National Historic Landmark in 1970 and has earned the distinction of being listed among the American Institute of Architects' ten greatest buildings in the country.

Burne-Jones Windows ①

Edward Burne-Jones' windows **(right)** – on the Boylston Street side – were inspired by the burgeoning English Arts and Crafts Movement. Its influence is readily apparent in his *David's Charge to Solomon*, with its bold patterning and rich colors.

② The Foundation

As part of Richardson's daring plan, the first of 4,500 wooden support pilings for the church was driven into the soggy Back Bay landfill in 1873. Reverend Phillips Brooks laid the cornerstone two years later.

③ Central Tower

The church's central tower borrows its square design from the Cathedral of Salamanca, in Spain. On the interior, wall paintings by La Farge depicting biblical figures in vibrant hues are in sharp contrast to the normally austere church interiors of the artist's day.

④ Front Facade and Side Towers

The Romanesque church of St Trophime in Arles, France, was the inspiration when Richardson redesigned Trinity's front portico, along with its two new side towers **(left)**. The additions were put in place by his firm of architects in the 1890s, after his death in 1886.

Interior of Trinity Church

⑤ Embroidered Kneelers

Trinity's colorful kneelers have been stitched by parishioners in memory of people and events past. They serve as an informal folk history of the congregation.

⑥ Pulpit Carving

Preachers from throughout the ages, including St. Paul, Martin Luther, and Phillips Brooks of Trinity, are depicted in high relief on the pulpit designed by Charles Coolidge.

Phillips Brooks' Bust 7

Keeping watch over the baptismal font is Rector Brooks **(right)**. Renowned for his bold sermons, he was rector at Trinity from 1869–91.

8 The Shop at Trinity

As well as religious books and items, the store also sells works inspired by the decorative details inside the church.

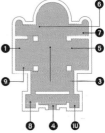

TRINITY SINGS "HALLELUJAH"

One of Boston's most cherished traditions is the singing of Handel's *Messiah*, with its rousing and unmistakable "Hallelujah Chorus," at Trinity during the Christmas season. Hundreds pack the sanctuary to experience the choir's ethereal, masterful treatment of the piece. Call 617 536 0944 for performance information.

10 Organ Pipes

The beautiful organ pipes frame the church's west wall. Exquisitely designed, ornately painted, and – of course – extremely sonorous, the pipes seem to hug the church's ceiling arches.

Church Floor Plan

9 La Farge Windows

A newcomer to stained glasswork at the time, John La Farge approached his commissions, such as the breathtaking *Christ in Majesty*, with the same sense of daring and vitality that architect Richardson employed in his Trinity design.

NEED TO KNOW

MAP L5 ■ 206 Clarendon St ■ "T" station: Copley Sq (green line) & Back Bay (orange line) ■ 617 536 0944 (church) ■ www.trinitychurchboston.org

Church: open for self-guided and audio tours: 10am–4:30pm Tue–Sat, after services–4:30pm Sun

Shop: open 10am–4:30pm Tue–Sat, as well as after services–4:30pm Sun

Guided and self-guided tours $10

....

■ Dine at Eataly *(see p93)* or the Prudential Center food court (800 Boylston St).

■ From September to June organ recitals are

held every Friday, 12:15–12:45pm.

■ Guided tours of the church are available and begin in the Welcome Center inside the Copley Square entrance.

■ A free guided tour is offered every Sunday following the last morning service.

TOP 10 ⭐ Isabella Stewart Gardner Museum

One needn't be a patron of the arts to be wowed by the Gardner Museum. Its namesake traveled tirelessly to acquire a world-class art collection, which is housed in a Venetian-style palazzo where flowers bloom, sculpted nudes pose in hidden corners, and entire ceilings reveal their European origins. The palace is complemented by a striking modern building, designed by Renzo Piano, which holds an intimate performance hall, galleries, and a charming café.

1 Titian Room

The most artistically significant gallery was conceived by Gardner as the palazzo's grand reception hall. It has an Italian flavor and showcases Cillini's *Bindo Altoviti* **(left)** and Titian's *Rape of Europa,* one of the most important paintings inspired by Ovid's *Metamorphoses*.

2 The Courtyard

Gardner integrated Roman, Byzantine, Romanesque, Renaissance, and Gothic elements in the magnificent courtyard **(right)**, which is out of bounds but can be viewed through the graceful arches surrounding it.

3 Long Gallery

Roman sculptural fragments and busts line glass cases that are filled with unusual 15th- and 16th-century books and artifacts. One such rare tome is a 1481 copy of Dante's *The Divine Comedy*, which features drawings by Botticelli.

4 Tapestry Room

Restored to its original 1914 state, this sweeping gallery houses two 16th-century Belgian tapestry cycles: one depicting *Scenes from the Life of Cyrus the Great* and the other *Scenes from the Life of Abraham*.

5 Dutch Room

Housing some of Gardner's most impressive Dutch and Flemish paintings, this room lost a Vermeer and three Rembrandts in a 1990 art heist that still remains unsolved.

6 Macknight, Yellow, and Blue Rooms

The Macknight, Yellow and Blue rooms **(left)** house portraits and sketches by Gardner's contemporaries such as, Manet, Matisse, Degas, and Sargent. Of particular note is Sargent's *Mrs Gardner in White*.

7 Gothic Room
John Singer Sargent's grand and somewhat risqué 1888 portrait of Mrs Gardner is here **(left)**, as well as medieval liturgical artwork from the 13th century.

8 Veronese Room
With its richly gilded and painted Spanish-leather wall-coverings, it's easy to miss this gallery's highlight: look up at Paolo Veronese's 16th-century master-work *The Coronation of Hebe*.

FENWAY COURT

Before Isabella Stewart Gardner died in 1924 she stipulated in her will that her home and her collection become a public museum. She believed that works of art should be displayed in a setting that would fire the imagination. So the collection, exhibited over three floors, is arranged purely to enhance the viewing of the individual treasures. To encourage visitors to respond to the artworks themselves, many of the 2,500 objects – from ancient Egyptian pieces to Matisse's paintings – are left unlabeled, as Gardner had requested.

Isabella Stewart Gardner Museum

Key to Floor Plan
- First floor
- Second floor
- Third floor

NEED TO KNOW

MAP D6 ■ 25 Evans Way ■ "T" station: Museum (green line/ E train) ■ 617 566 1401 ■ www. gardnermuseum.org

Open 11am–5pm Wed–Mon (to 9pm Thu)

Adm $10–$15; free for under 17s and anyone named Isabella

■ Light salads and sandwiches are served in the museum's café.

■ The museum's Calderwood Hall hosts classical as well as contemporary music concerts. See website for details.

■ On the third Thursday of every month, the museum hosts creative studio projects as well as live music, dance and performance art.

9 Spanish Cloister
With stunning mosaic tiling and a Moorish arch, the Spanish Cloister looks like a hidden patio at the Alhambra. But Sargent's sweeping *El Jaleo* (1882), all sultry shadows and rich hues, gives the room its distinctiveness.

10 Raphael Room
Gardner was the first collector to bring works by Raphael to the US; three of his major works are here, alongside Botticelli's *Tragedy of Lucretia* and Crivelli's *St. George and Slaying the Dragon*.

🔟 ⭐ Charlestown Navy Yard

Some of the most storied battleships in American naval history began life at Charlestown Navy Yard. Established in 1800 as one of the country's first naval yards, Charlestown remained vital to US security until its decommissioning in 1974. From the wooden-hulled USS *Constitution* built in 1797 to the World War II steel destroyer USS *Cassin Young*, the yard gives visitors an all-hands-on-deck historical experience unparalleled in America.

1 USS Constitution

First tested in action during the War of 1812, the USS *Constitution* **(above)** is the world's oldest warship still afloat. A tugboat helps her perform an annual turnaround cruise on July 4th.

4 USS Cassin Young

Never defeated, despite withstanding multiple kamikaze bomber-attacks in the Pacific, this World War II era destroyer **(right)** could be considered USS *Constitution's* 20th-century successor.

2 Navy Yard Visitor Center

Begin your stroll through the yard at the National Park Service-operated Visitor Center, where you can pick up literature about the site's many attractions and check on tour schedules.

3 Bunker Hill Monument

This 220-ft (67-m) granite obelisk **(right)**, near the yard has towered over Charlestown since 1842. It was built to commemorate the first major battle of the American Revolution *(see p14)*.

5 Commandant's House

The oldest building in the yard, dating from 1805, housed the command-ants of the First Naval District. With its sweeping harbor views and wrap-around veranda, this elegant mansion was ideal for entertaining dignitaries from all over the world.

6 Dry Dock #1

To facilitate hull repairs, Dry Dock #1 **(left)** was opened in 1833. It was drained by massive steam-powered pumps. USS *Constitution* was the first ship to be given an overhaul here.

7 Ropewalk

This quarter-mile- (0.5-km-) long building (1837) houses steam-powered machinery that produced rope rigging for the nation's warships.

8 USS Constitution Museum

With activities to keep kids entertained, as well as enough nautical trivia and artifacts – from muskets **(above)** to spoils of war – to satisfy a naval historian, this museum brings to life USS *Constitution*'s two centuries of service.

9 Muster House

This octagonal brick building was designed in the Georgian-revival style popular in the northeast in the mid 19th century. The house served as an administration hub, where the yard's clerical work was carried out.

10 Marine Railway

The Navy Yard has constantly evolved to meet changing demands and developments. The marine railway was built in 1918 to haul submarines and other vessels out of the water for hull repairs.

Map of Charlestown Navy Yard

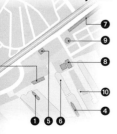

OLD IRONSIDES

Given her 25-inch- (63-cm-) thick hull at the waterline, it's easy to imagine why USS *Constitution* earned her nickname "Old Ironsides." Pitted against HMS *Guerriere* during the War of 1812, the ship engaged in a shoot-out that left *Guerriere* all but destroyed. Seeing British cannon balls "bouncing" off USS *Constitution*'s hull, a sailor allegedly exclaimed, "Huzzah! Her sides are made of iron." The rest is history.

NEED TO KNOW

MAP H2 ■ "T" station: North Station (green & orange lines) ■ Water shuttle from Long Wharf; www.mbta.com

Naval Yard Visitor Center: Building Number 5; 617 242 5601; open times vary, call to check; www.nps.gov/bost

Bunker Hill Monument, USS Cassin Young, USS Constitution: open times vary, check website for details; www.nps.gov/bost

USS Constitution Museum: open Apr–Oct: 9am–6pm daily; Nov–Mar: 10am–5pm daily ■ Donation

······································

■ Try some pub grub at the atmospheric Warren Tavern (2 Pleasant St).

■ Photo ID (18 and up) and metal screening required to board the USS *Constitution*.

TOP 10 ⭐ New England Aquarium

The sea pervades nearly every aspect of Boston life, so it's only appropriate that the New England Aquarium is one of the city's most popular attractions. What sets this aquarium apart from many similar institutions is its commitment not only to presenting an exciting environment to learn about marine life, but also to conserving the natural habitats of its thousands of gilled, feathered, and whiskered inhabitants.

Penguin Exhibit ①

Three species of penguins – southern Rockhoppers, Little Blue, and African – coexist here, frolicking on the central island **(right)** and taking dips in the pool.

② Yawkey Coral Reef Center

This exhibit reveals a closeup look at species found inhabiting the coral reefs of the Caribbean, including long-spined sea urchins and gently swaying garden eels that burrow together in colonies.

⑤ Marine Mammal Center

Observe Northern fur seals as they frolic in an open-air exhibit at the edge of the Boston Harbor. Meet the seals and sea lions face-to-face at the large observation deck.

③ Edge of the Sea

For those not content to merely gaze at fish behind glass, the Edge of the Sea tidepool tank puts marine life at visitors' fingertips – literally. Inside a ground-level fiberglass tank, the New England seashore is recreated in all its diversity.

④ Atlantic Harbor Seal Exhibit

Harbor seals **(below)** swim, feed, and play in specially designed tanks outside the aquarium. All have either been born in captivity or rescued and deemed unfit for release into the wild.

⑥ Pacific Reef

A Pacific coral reef teems with brightly colored inhabitants **(above)**, including unicorn tangs, bird wrasses, and blue-striped cleaner fish, in tanks, filled with painted artificial coral. Children will love spotting the blue palette surgeon-fish – the forgetful Dory in *Finding Nemo*.

7 Giant Ocean Tank

Displaying a spectacular four-story Caribbean reef, the Giant Ocean Tank (above) teems with sea turtles, sharks, moray eels, brightly colored tropical fish, and scores of other species in its 200,000-gallon (900,000-liter) space.

9 Whale Watch

The aquarium's whale watch catamarans, running mid-March to mid-November, offer a unique glimpse into the life cycles of the world's largest mammals. The swift boats voyage far outside Boston Harbor to the Stellwagen Bank, a prime feeding area for whales.

10 Gulf of Maine

This six-tank exhibit shows New England's marine and seashore environments inhabited by giant sea stars, sharp-clawed crustaceans, and cold water fish such as cod, halibut, and dogfish.

THE AQUARIUM'S MISSION

The aquarium's aim, first and foremost, is to instigate and support marine conservation. Its Conservation Action Fund has fought on behalf of endangered marine animals worldwide, helping to protect humpback whales in the South Pacific, sea turtles in New England, and dolphins in Peru.

NEED TO KNOW

MAP R3 ■ Central Wharf ■ 617 973 5200 ■ "T" station: Aquarium (blue line) ■ www.neaq.org for general info, including current IMAX® features

Open 9am–5pm Mon–Fri, 9am–6pm Sat & Sun (extended hours Jul–Aug)

Adm adults $27.95; seniors $25.95; children (aged 3–11) $18.95; under 3s free

Whale Watch: 617 973 5206 for reservations and rate information

IMAX: call 866 815 IMAX (4629) for show times; Adm: adults $9.95; seniors and children (aged 3–11) $7.95

■ If the aquarium has not convinced you to remove fish from your diet, visit Legal Harborside for a moderately priced meal *(see p64)*. Quick, quality bites from around the globe can also be had at the Quincy Market food hall, three blocks away.

■ Purchase discount combo tickets for the aquarium along with an IMAX film or a whale-watching excursion.

8 Shark and Ray Touch Tank

One of the largest of its kind in the country, this mangrove-themed tank (above) has shallow edges and viewing windows, allowing visitors to roll up their sleeves to feel the velvety wings of stingrays and the abrasive skin of sharks.

Key to Floor Plan
■ First floor
■ Second floor
■ Third floor

New England Aquarium

The Top 10
of Everything

**Northern Avenue Bridge
and skyscrapers**

Moments in History	42	Bars	60
Figures in Boston's History	44	Restaurants	62
Waterfront Areas	46	Spots for Seafood	64
Boston Harbor Islands	48	Cafés	66
Off the Beaten Path	50	Essential Shopping Experiences	68
Children's Attractions	52	Boston for Free	70
Performing Arts Venues	54	Festivals and Events	72
Dance and Live Music Venues	56	Day Trips: Historic New England	74
Gay and Lesbian Hangouts	58	Day Trips: The Beach	76

☷☰ Moments in History

Battle of Concord Bridge, 1775

1 1630: Boston Founded

Under the leadership of John Winthrop *(see p44)*, English Puritans moved from overcrowded Charlestown and colonized the Shawmut Peninsula. Permission was granted from its sole English inhabitant, Anglican cleric William Blaxton. Their city on the hill was named Boston in honor of the native English town of their leaders.

2 1636: Harvard Created

Boston's Puritan leaders established a college at Newtowne (later Cambridge) to educate future generations of clergy. When young Charlestown minister John Harvard died two years later and left his books and half his money to the college, it was renamed Harvard in his memory *(see p20)*.

Carved detail, Boston Public Library

3 1775: American Revolution

Friction between colonists and the British Crown had been building for more than a decade when British troops marched on Lexington to confiscate rebel weapons. Forewarned by Paul Revere *(see p44)*, local militia, known as the Minute Men, skirmished with British regulars on Lexington Green. During the second confrontation at Concord, "the shot heard round the world" marked the beginning of the Revolution, which ended in American independence with the 1783 Treaty of Paris.

4 1845: Irish Arrived

Irish citizens, fleeing the devastating potato famine in their country, arrived in Boston in tens of thousands, many eventually settling in the south of the city. By 1900, the Irish were the dominant ethnic group in Boston. They flexed their political muscle accordingly, culminating in the election of John F. Kennedy *(see p45)* as president in 1960.

5 1848: Boston Public Library Founded

The Boston Public Library was established as the first publicly supported municipal library in the US. In 1895 the library moved into the Italianate "palace of the people" on Copley Square *(see p87)*.

6 1863: Black Boston Went to War

Following decades of agitation to abolish slavery, the city sent the country's first African-American regiment to join Union forces in the Civil War. The regiment was honored by the Shaw Memorial on Boston Common *(see p18)*.

7 1897: Subway Opened

The Tremont Street subway, the first underground in the US, was opened on September 1 to ease road congestion. It cost $4.4 million to construct and the initial fare was five cents. The Massachusetts Bay Transportation Authority (MBTA) now transports 1.2 million people daily.

8 1958: Freedom Trail Opened

This historical walking tour connects the city's sights. It was based on a 1951 *Boston Herald Traveler* column by William Scofield, and was the first of its kind in the US *(see p12)*.

Zakim Bridge, part of the Big Dig

9 2007: The Big Dig

The $15 billion highway project to alleviate traffic congestion was completed in 2007, leaving in its place the Rose Kennedy Greenway Park and the soaring Zakim Bridge, the world's widest cable-stayed bridge.

Boston Marathon bombing tributes

10 2013: Boston Marathon Bombing

On April 15, 2013, two terrorist bombs exploded near the finish line of the Boston Marathon, killing three people and injuring 264. Following the attack, one bomber was killed in an encounter with the police; the other was convicted and sentenced to death in 2015.

TOP 10 INNOVATIONS

1 Sewing Machine
Elias Howe invented the sewing machine in Cambridge in 1845, but spent decades securing patent rights.

Howe's sewing machine

2 Surgical Anesthesia
Ether was first used to anesthetize patients at Massachusetts General Hospital in 1846.

3 Telephone
Alexander Graham Bell invented the telephone in his Boston laboratory in 1876.

4 Safety Razor
Bostonian King Camp Gillette invented the safety razor with disposable blades in 1901.

5 Mutual Fund
Massachusetts Investors Trust opened in 1924 as the first modern mutual fund that pooled investors' money to purchase portfolio stocks.

6 Programmable Digital Computer
A Harvard team built the first programmable digital computer, Mark 1, in 1946. Its 750,000 components weighed about 10,000 lb (454 kg).

7 Microwave Oven
A Raytheon company engineer placed popcorn in front of a radar tube in 1946 and discovered the principle behind the microwave oven.

8 Instant Film
Cambridge, Massachusetts, inventor Edwin Land devised the Polaroid camera, launched in 1948.

9 Email
Ray Tomlinson, an engineer at Bolt, Beranek, and Newman in Cambridge, sent the first email message in 1971.

10 Facebook
Harvard student Mark Zuckerberg posted the first message to Facemash (social network site Facebook's predecessor) in 2003.

Figures in Boston's History

1 John Winthrop (1587–1649)

Acting on a daring plan put together by English Puritans in 1629, John Winthrop led approximately 800 settlers to the New World to build a godly civilization in the wilderness. He settled his Puritan charges at Boston in 1630 [see p42] and served as governor of the Massachusetts Bay Colony until his death.

John Winthrop

2 Increase Mather (1639–1723)

Harvard-educated preacher Increase Mather solidified the hold of Puritan theologians on Massachusetts. When William III took the English Crown, Mather persuaded the king to grant a charter that gave the colony the right to elect the council of the governor in 1691. His influence was later undermined by his support of the 1692 Salem witch trials.

Samuel Adams

3 Samuel Adams (1722–1803)

Failed businessman Samuel Adams became Boston's master politician in the eventful years leading up to the Revolution [see p14]. Adams signed the Declaration of Independence and served in both of the Continental Congresses. He later became the governor of Massachusetts, and joined Paul Revere to lay the cornerstone of the State House [see p15] in 1795.

4 Paul Revere (1735–1818)

Best known for his "midnight ride" to forewarn the rebels of the British march on Concord, Revere served the American Revolution as organizer, messenger, and propagandist. A gifted silversmith with many pieces in the Museum of Fine Arts [see p28–31], he founded the metalworking firm that gilded the State House dome and sheathed the hull of the USS *Constitution*.

5 Harrison Gray Otis (1765–1848)

In the 1790s, Harrison Gray Otis and James Mason transformed Beacon Hill from a hilly pasture into a chic neighborhood that embodies the Federal building style. Otis championed the architecture of Charles Bulfinch, and three of his Bulfinch-designed houses still grace Beacon Hill, including the one now known as Harrison Gray Otis House [see p82].

6 Donald McKay (1810–1880)

McKay built the largest and swiftest of the great clipper ships in his East Boston shipyard in 1850. The speedy vessels revolutionized long-distance shipping at the time of the California gold rush and gave Boston its last glory days as a mercantile port before the rise of rail transportation.

7 Mary Baker Eddy (1821–1910)

After recovering from a major accident, Eddy wrote *Science and Health with Key to the Scriptures*, the basis of Christian Science. She founded a church in Boston in 1879, and in 1892 reorganized it as the First Church of Christ, Scientist (see p88). Eddy also established the Pulitzer prize-winning *Christian Science Monitor* newspaper in 1908.

8 James Michael Curley (1874–1958)

Self-proclaimed champion of "the little people," Curley used patronage and Irish pride to retain a stranglehold on Boston politics from his election as mayor in 1914 until his defeat at the polls in 1949. Known as "the rascal king" he embodied political corruption but created many enduring public works.

James Michael Curley

9 John F. Kennedy (1917–1963)

Grandson of Irish-American mayor John "Honey Fitz" Fitzgerald and son of ambassador Joseph Kennedy, John F. Kennedy represented Boston in both houses of the US Congress before he became the first Roman Catholic elected president of the United States. The presidential library at Columbia Point recounts the story of his brief, but intense, period in office (see p133).

10 W. Arthur Garrity, Jr. (1920–1999)

In 1974, US District Court judge Garrity ruled that African-American students had been denied their constitutional rights to the best available education. His desegregation plan for Boston's 200 schools set off protests, some violent, in predominantly white neighborhoods.

LITERARY BOSTONIANS

Dorothy West

1 Anne Bradstreet
Bradstreet (c.1612–72) was America's first poet, publishing *The Tenth Muse, Lately Sprung Up in America* in 1650.

2 Ralph Waldo Emerson
Poet and philosopher Emerson (1803–82) espoused transcendentalism as well as pioneering American literary independence.

3 Henry Wadsworth Longfellow
Known for epic poems such as *Hiawatha*, Longfellow (1807–82) also translated Dante.

4 Louisa May Alcott
Little Women sealed the literary fame of Alcott (1832–88), but she also acted as a nurse in the Civil War.

5 Henry James
Master of sonorous prose, James (1843–1916) is considered one of the creators of the psychological novel.

6 Dorothy West
African-American novelist and essayist, West (1907–98) made sharp observations about class and race conflicts.

7 Robert Lowell
The "confessional poetry" of Lowell (1917–77) went on to influence a whole generation of writers.

8 Robert Parker
Scholar of mystery literature, Parker (1932–2010) is best known for his signature detective Spenser.

9 Robert Pinsky
Poet, critic, and translator, Pinsky (b.1940) served as US poet laureate and now teaches at Boston University.

10 Dennis Lehane
Novelist Dennis Lehane (b.1965) brings a dark, tragic vision to the working-class neighborhoods of Boston.

TOP10 Waterfront Areas

Sailing boats on the Esplanade

1 The Esplanade
MAP M3

Provided the Charles River Basin has not frozen over, collegiate rowing crews, canoeists, small sailboats, and the occasional coast guard patrol all share the waters off the Esplanade. Find a bench facing the water and take in the scene.

2 Castle Island Reservation
2010 Day Blvd, South Boston
617 727 5290

Connected to the mainland via an earthen causeway and crowned by the c.1851 Fort Independence, Castle Island is New England's oldest continually fortified site *(see p132)*. Aside from exploring the fort's bunkers and tunnels (in season), visitors enjoy fine panoramic views of Boston Harbor.

3 Constitution Beach
Bennington St, East Boston

Views of Downtown don't get much better than those from this tastefully revitalized beach and park area in East Boston. A clean beach, picnic areas, and lifeguards make this a favorite with families.

4 Long Wharf
MAP R2

Long Wharf has been indispensable to Boston's merchant industry for over 300 years. Given the wharf's deep frontage and proximity to waterfront warehouses, the biggest ships of their day could dock here. Today, ferry services and cruise vessels depart from here, creating a spirited dock scene, and there's excellent waterside dining at a branch of the restaurant Legal Sea Foods.

5 Fish Pier

By 1926 – 12 years after its construction – the Greco-Roman style Commonwealth Pier (aka Fish Pier) had become the world's busiest and largest fish market. The day's catch is still brought to the early morning market here. Sample some of it in hearty chowders at the legendary No Name Restaurant *(see p65)*.

6 Fort Point Channel
MAP H5

Fort Point has lured artists to the neighborhood with affordable studio space in old warehouse buildings. Open studios in May and October offer a peek inside and a chance to bag a bargain on artwork. Where artists go, gentrification is sure to follow: the neighborhood now boasts the $300-million Federal Courthouse and trendy cafés and restaurants.

Boats on the Fort Point Channel

7 Christopher Columbus Park
MAP P2

Featuring an Italian marble sculpture of the seafaring colonizer, Christopher Columbus Park is among the North End's best-kept secrets. Vine-encrusted arches, manicured gardens, and sweeping harbor and skyline views make this a place to linger.

Swanky Rowes Wharf

8 Rowes Wharf
MAP R3

Framed by the colossal atrium of the Boston Harbor Hotel *(see p146)*, Rowes Wharf is a popular docking spot for the high-end harbor cruise outfits and is a luxurious contrast to the city's grittier, saltier working docks. The hotel sponsors free concerts and film screenings on summer evenings.

9 Puopolo Park
MAP H2

North End's Puopolo Park boasts supreme frontage on the harbor, looking out toward Charlestown. On warm days, the neighborhood's old guard enjoys a game of *bocce* (bowls). Nearby, kids play baseball or splash around in the outdoor pool.

10 Charles River Locks and Dam
MAP F2

This dam controls water levels in the basin below and maintains separation of the river from the harbor. A series of locks permits boats to pass from one body of water to the other.

TOP 10 VIEWS

Weeks Footbridge

1 Weeks Footbridge
MAP B2
A prime spectator spot during the Head of the Charles Regatta *(see p73)*.

2 Longfellow Bridge
MAP M2
The entire Charles River Basin becomes your oyster on the "T" between Kendall and Charles/MGH stops.

3 Bunker Hill Monument
Climb to the capstone to see all of Charlestown, Cambridge, and Boston laid out before you *(see p36)*.

4 Spirit of Boston Cruises
World Trade Center ▪ 866 310 2469
Admire the city from the water as you enjoy brunch, lunch, drinks, or dinner

5 Charlestown Bridge
MAP G2
This bridge offers splendid harbor and Downtown vistas.

6 John J. Moakley Courthouse Park
This beautiful waterfront park has fine views of the towering Financial District.

7 Hyatt Regency Cambridge
MAP C4 ▪ 575 Memorial Drive, Cambridge ▪ 617 492 1234
Gaze across the river from the seasonal patio at Zephyr on the Charles.

8 Prudential Skywalk
Jaw-dropping panoramic views from a 50th-floor observatory *(see p53)*.

9 Dorchester Heights Monument
MAP Q3 ▪ 15 State S
The park around this commemorative spire offers broad views of the harbor.

10 Hyatt Regency Boston Harbor
101 Harborside Drive, East Boston ▪ 617 568 1234
The Hyatt's Harborside Grill and Patio boasts panoramic Boston views.

🔟 Boston Harbor Islands

1 Deer Island

Accessed by a causeway attaching the island to the mainland, part of the island was opened in 2006 for recreation and walking – with dramatic views of the Boston skyline. Deer Island is also known for its impressive, state-of-the-art $3.8 billion sewage treatment plant. Distinguished by 12 gigantic egg-shaped digesters, it was key to cleaning up Boston Harbor.

Church on Peddocks Island

2 Peddocks Island

Peddocks is one of Boston Harbor's largest and most diverse islands. Hiking trails circle a pond, salt marsh, and coastal forest, and pass by Fort Andrews, which was active in harbor defense from 1904 through to World War II. The island is known for the beach plums and wild roses which bloom profusely in the dunes. A visitor center and campsite make it an overnight destination.

3 Lovells Island

Known for its extensive dunes, Lovells also has an unsupervised swimming beach. Extensive hiking trails lead across the dunes and through woodlands. The remains of Fort Standish, which was active during the Spanish American War and World War I, can also be explored.

4 Grape and Bumpkin Islands

Both these islands are a delight for naturalists – Bumpkin for its wildflowers, raspberries, and bayberries, and Grape for its wild roses and bird life. On Bumpkin Island, hiking trails pass the ruins of a farmhouse and 19th-century children's hospital, which also housed German prisoners rescued from Boston Harbor in World War I and later polio patients, before burning down in 1945.

5 Georges Island

Islands open May–Oct (information booth at Long Wharf) ▪ 617 223 8666 ▪ www.boston harborislands.org

As the terminal for the harbor islands ferry and water shuttles to other islands, Georges Island is the gateway to the Boston Harbor Islands National Park Area, which includes 34 islands and mainland parks. Visitors can hike, explore historic buildings, view birds, and watch the passing ships. But it is also worth spending time here to visit the Civil-War-era Fort Warren and check out the snack bar and gift shop.

6 Spectacle Island

Vastly enlarged by fill from the Big Dig (see p43), Spectacle Island has some of the highest peaks of the harbor islands and the best Boston skyline view. The construction of a café and visitor center has made it one of the most popular of all the harbor islands. Visitors can enjoy 5 miles (8 km) of trails and swimming beaches with lifeguards.

The scenic Spectacle Island

Little Brewster Island, with its historic lighthouse

(7) Little Brewster Island

Island closed due to storm damage, call for details ▪ 617 223 8666 ▪ Adm

Boston Light, the first US lighthouse, was constructed here in 1716 and it remains the last staffed offshore lighthouse in the country. Limited tours visit the small museum and lead visitors up the 76 spiral steps and two ladders to reach the top.

(8) Gallops Island

Once the site of a popular summer resort, Gallops also served as quarters for Civil War soldiers, including the Massachusetts 54th Regiment *(see p18)*. The island has an extensive sandy beach, a picnic area, hiking paths, and historic ruins of a former quarantine and immigration station. The Massachusetts Department of Conservation and Recreation has closed the island indefinitely for a thorough environmental clean up.

(9) Thompson Island

Open Jun–Aug: Sat & Sun ▪ 617 328 3900 ▪ Ferries depart from EDIC Pier off Summer Street ▪ Adm

A learning center since the 1830s, Thompson is the site of an Outward Bound program serving more than 5,000 students annually. The island's diverse geography includes rocky and sandy shores, a large salt marsh, sumac groves, and a hardwood forest. Killdeer, herons, and shorebirds abound.

(10) World's End

Operated by Trustees of Reservations: 1 781 740 6665 ▪ Adm for non-members

This 0.4-sq-mile (1-sq-km) peninsula overlooking Hingham Bay is a geological sibling of the harbor islands, with its two glacial drumlins, rocky beaches, ledges, cliffs, and both salt- and freshwater marshes. Frederick Law Olmsted *(see p19)* laid out the grounds for a homestead development here in the late 19th century. The homes were never built, but carriage paths, formal plantings, and hedgerows remain. World's End is accessed by road by driving through Hingham.

🔟 Off the Beaten Path

Sports Museum of New England

1 Sports Museum of New England

MAP P1 ■ TD Garden, 100 Legends Way ■ 617 624 1234 ■ Open 10am–4pm Mon–Sat, 11am–4pm Sun; closed on event days, see website ■ Adm ■ www.sportsmuseum.org

Spread over two floors above the TD Garden, home of the Bruins (ice hockey) and Celtics (basketball), are displays on all the city's renowned teams. The collection includes items such as a section of the old wooden seats from the original Boston Garden, where you can sit and watch historic games on a big screen.

2 Longfellow House and Washington's Headquarters

In 1775–6, the Federal house served as George Washington's headquarters during the siege of Boston. Over half a century later it was home to legendary American poet Henry Wadsworth Longfellow and his family (see p124).

3 Captain Jackson's Historic Chocolate Shop

MAP Q1 ■ Clough House, 21 Unity St ■ 617 858 8231 ■ Opening hours vary; see website for details ■ www. oldnorth.com/captainjacksons

This shop explores the history of chocolate making during the American colonial period. Engaging demonstrations, conducted daily, illustrate how chocolate was produced in the 18th century. Visitors can also purchase chocolate blocks and coffee.

4 Mapparium

MAP K6 ■ 200 Massachusetts Ave ■ 617 450 7000 ■ Open 10am–4pm Tue–Sun ■ Adm ■ www.mary bakereddylibrary.org

The oddly fascinating Mapparium is a stained-glass globe the size of a large room that you view from the inside as you stroll through it along a glass walkway. Illuminated by LED lighting, the countries represented on the globe's surface are those that existed when it was built in 1935. Fabulous acoustics allow whispers to be heard at opposite ends of the space. The Mapparium is located in the Mary Baker Eddy Library, which also features a small museum dedicated to Eddy and the Christian Science religion she founded (see p44–5).

Stained-glass Mapparium

5 The New England Holocaust Memorial

MAP Q4 ■ Between Congress and Union Sts

Six luminous, glass towers soar above a black granite path bordered by lawns and trees. The structures represent the six main death camps and the six million Jews who died during the six years of World War II.

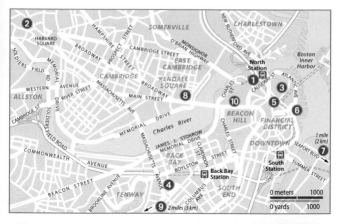

6 Ghosts and Gravestones
MAP R3 ■ 200 Atlantic Ave
■ 866 754 9136 ■ Adm ■ www.
ghostsandgravestones.com
Hop on the black trolley of doom
with a gravedigger guide for a
"frightseeing" tour of the city's
most haunted spots, and visit
the site of New England's greatest
grave-robbing scandal.

7 The Lawn on D
420 D St ■ 877 393 3393
■ Open dawn to dusk ■ www.
signatureboston.com/lawn-on-d
One of Boston's newest and most
popular green spaces, The Lawn
on D is located in the heart of the
Seaport District and is close to the
Convention and Exhibition Center.
This hip outdoor space features live
music, lawn games, and food trucks.

8 Paddle the Charles River
MAP E3 ■ Charles River Canoe and
Kayak, Broad Canal Way, Kendall
Square, Cambridge ■ 617 965 5110
■ Adm ■ www.paddleboston.com
What better way to get a whole
new perspective on Boston than by
seeing it from the water? Visitors
can rent their own canoe, kayak,
and paddleboard or even join a tour
with a larger group. Options on offer
include Skyline, Sunset, and Boston
Harbor tours (by kayak only).

Interior of Samuel Adams Brewery

9 Samuel Adams Brewery
30 Germania St ■ 617 368 5080
■ Tours www.samueladams.com
The lively tour of the Samuel Adams
craft brewery takes you through
the process and offers free tastings
of Samuel Adams' famous beers.
Note that the tours can't be booked
in advance as the tickets are sold
on a first-come-first-serve basis.

10 Paul S. Russell, MD Museum of Medical History and Innovation
MAP N2 ■ Massachusetts General
Hospital, 2 North Grove St ■ 617 724
8009 ■ Open 9am–5pm Mon–Fri, also
Apr–Oct: 11am–5pm Sat ■ www.
massgeneral.org/museum
This museum traces medical innovation with displays, artifacts, and
guides. The Ether Dome, nearby,
was the site of the first successful
use of ether anesthetic in surgery.

⓾ Children's Attractions

Exhibit in the Children's Museum

① Children's Museum

This venerable funhouse *(see p96)* pioneered the interactive-exhibit concept now found in museums worldwide. It includes a climbing wall, a Big Dig-style *(see p43)* construction zone, and a science playground where tracks, balls, and bubbles encourage kids to investigate, and make learning fun. The museum runs a program of special events throughout the year covering a range of subjects, including health, engineering, and literacy.

Boston Duck Tours

② Museum of Science

Hands-on learning exhibits, such as assembling animal skeletons or building a computer model, teach children the thrill of discovery. The Omni Theater delights with its fast-paced IMAX projections, while the planetarium places the cosmos within reach. There are also 4-D film presentations and a butterfly garden *(see pp16–17)*.

③ Swan Boats

MAP N4 ▪ Public Garden ▪ 617 522 1966 ▪ Open mid-Apr–mid-Sep: usually 10am–5pm daily ▪ Adm

If Boston were to have a mascot, it would likely sport white feathers and a graceful, arching neck. The swan boats *(see p19)* have been a Public Garden fixture since the first fleet glided onto the pond here in 1877.

④ Boston Duck Tours

MAP K6 ▪ Prudential Center, New England Aquarium, and Museum of Science ▪ 617 267 3825 ▪ Open mid-Mar–Nov: 9am–dusk daily ▪ Adm ▪ www.bostonduck tours.com

Board a World War II-style amphibious vehicle that plies the Charles River as smoothly as it navigates Back Bay streets. This historic tour encompasses the entire peninsula and is conducted by informative and entertaining guides.

⑤ New England Aquarium

The aquarium *(see pp38–9)* goes to great lengths to keep kids entertained through a variety of interactive displays. Nothing illustrates this better than the Edge of the Sea exhibit, where children can touch some of the region's typical tidepool dwellers.

Loggerhead sea turtle at the New England Aquarium

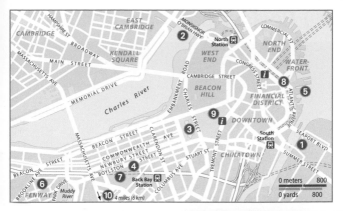

6 Fenny Park

Fenway Park

For children with even the slightest interest in sports, a Red Sox game at legendary Fenway Park *(see p117)* is pure magic. It is impossible for fans not to feel part of the action at the country's most intimate professional baseball park.

7 Prudential Skywalk
MAP K6 ▪ 800 Boylston St ▪ 617 859 0648 ▪ Open Mar–Oct: 10am–10pm daily; Nov–Feb: 10am–8pm daily ▪ Adm

Located on the 50th floor of the Prudential Tower *(see p88)*, this observatory provides a rewarding Boston geography lesson. Should the jaw-dropping, 360° views not keep the youngsters enthralled, the audio guide to Boston's history will. The swift, ear-popping elevator ride to the top is also a thrill.

8 Greenway Carousel
MAP P1 ▪ Rose Kennedy Greenway ▪ www.rosekennedy greenway.org

Set inside the Rose Kennedy Greenway, the linear green parkland in the heart of Boston, this charming seasonal carousel features hand-carved figures of 14 local animals, including a squirrel, turtle, cod, lobster, whale, harbor seal, skunk, 3 types of butterfly, and more. It is also accessible to individuals with disabilities.

Frog statue beside Frog Pond

9 Frog Pond
MAP M4 ▪ Boston Common

As soon as temperatures dip below freezing, kids flock to quaint Frog Pond *(see p18)* for ice skating and hot chocolate at the adjacent hut. Boston's oft-oppressive summer days lure them back for splashing and fun beneath the central fountain.

10 Franklin Park Zoo
1 Franklin Park Rd, Dorchester ▪ 617 541 5466 ▪ Open 10am–5pm Mon–Fri, 10am–6pm Sat–Sun (Oct–Mar: 10am–4pm daily) ▪ Adm ▪ www.zoonewengland.com

Boston's urban zoo, dating back to 1913, houses over 200 species of animals. Its Tropical Forest section houses gorillas, leopards, and other exotic creatures. Bird's World show-cases and provides a safe environment for dozens of species. The seasonal Franklin Farm lets kids get close to domestic farm animals.

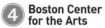 Performing Arts Venues

Boston Pops Orchestra playing at the Symphony Hall

1 Symphony Hall

Opened in 1900, Symphony Hall was designed by a Harvard physics professor Wallace Clement Sabine and is one of the world's most acoustically perfect concert venues. It is home to the internationally renowned Boston Symphony Orchestra and the Boston Pops (see p117). The BSO commissions new works, hosts world premieres, and frequently welcomes sought-after guest conductors and soloists.

2 Boch Center – Wang Theatre

Capturing the gilded and marbled opulence of its muse, Versailles, the 3,500-seat Wang ranks among the city's most beautiful buildings (see p107). The Wang hosts touring productions from Broadway and London's West End as well as dance and opera productions by local companies.

3 Hatch Shell

MAP M3 ◼ The Esplanade
◼ 617 635 4505

Constructed in 1941, this shell around a performance stage projects music across the Esplanade. Every Fourth of July (see p73) the Boston Pops Orchestra rings in Independence Day here. Free Friday Flicks (see p70) brings firm family faves such as *The Wizard of Oz* and *Frozen* to the screen, while dance and music events occur almost nightly during summer.

4 Boston Center for the Arts

Home to three theater companies, four stages, and a gallery, the BCA is the cornerstone of the South End arts scene (see p107). The artists who perform and exhibit here present some of the city's most provocative work. The Cyclorama, at the heart of the BCA, was built in 1884 to house a 360-degree painting of the Battle of Gettysburg.

The historic Somerville Theatre

5 Somerville Theatre

55 Davis Sq, Somerville
◼ 617 625 5700 ◼ www.somerville theatreonline.com

Extensive renovation has returned this Davis Square landmark to its original, ornate glory. When it isn't hosting some of the country's finest jazz, world music, and underground rock acts, the Somerville packs audiences in for feature films at low ticket prices.

6 New England Conservatory, Jordan Hall

MAP E6 ■ 30 Gainsborough St ■ 617 585 1260 ■ www.necmusic.edu

Dozens of local orchestral and choral ensembles call the NEC's Jordan Hall home. Built at the turn of the 20th century and renowned for its intimacy and impressive acoustics, the hall hosts more than 450 free concerts a year.

7 Boston Opera House

MAP G4 ■ 539 Washington St ■ 617 259 3400 ■ www.bostonopera house.com

The Boston Opera House was one of the city's most ornate movie palaces when it opened in 1928. With a $54 million renovation in 2004, the theater was returned to its former glory, and today it presents a steady stream of mostly Broadway shows and is also the home of the Boston Ballet.

8 TD Garden

MAP G2 ■ 100 Legends Way ■ 617 624 1050 ■ www.tdgarden.com

Seating almost 20,000 and with over 3.5 million visitors a year, this arena is home to the NBA's Boston Celtics and the NHL's Boston Bruins, plus the Sports Museum of New England (see p50). It offers a full schedule of concerts, family entertainment, ice shows, public and sporting events.

Berklee Performance Center

9 Berklee Performance Center

Berklee, the world's largest independent music college, boasts this premier venue. The great acoustics ensure that some of the most highly distinguished jazz, folk, and world musicians play here (see p89). The student performances held here are usually free and among the best entertainment deals in town.

10 Sanders Theatre

MAP B1 ■ 45 Quincy St, Cambridge ■ 617 496 2222

Located in Harvard's splendid Memorial Hall (see p20), this theater has hosted many luminaries over its 120-plus years. Great performers of the past century have graced its intimate stage, including mime artist Marcel Marceau. Longfellow, Oliver Wendell Holmes, and Ralph Wardo Emerson were among its early audiences.

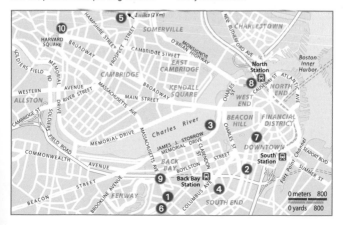

⊞ Dance and Live Music Venues

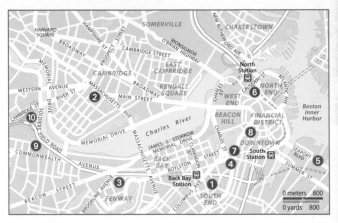

① The Beehive

The nightly music mix here might sometimes veer toward cabaret or even burlesque, but local jazz musicians are the mainstay for a usually well-dressed, mature crowd at least a decade past their school-days. A convivial bar scene and excellent contemporary bistro fare round out the appeal of this great night out *(see p111)*.

② The Middle East

The region's alternative rock scene can trace its genesis to this Central Square landmark. This influential venue has launched many careers. Seminal local bands like the Pixies, Mighty Mighty Bosstones, and Morphine all played on The Middle East's three stages. Today, the club *(see p128)* continues the tradition, genuinely embracing musicians operating just under the mainstream radar.

③ House of Blues
MAP D5 ▪ 15 Lansdowne St ▪ 888 693 2583 ▪ Adm

The House of Blues chain was born across the river in Cambridge, and this 2,400-capacity room behind Fenway Park continues the commitment to American

music: blues, gospel, jazz, rhythm and blues, and roots-based rock 'n' roll. A Gospel brunch is offered occasionally, and the restaurant also opens during Red Sox evening home games.

Decor at the House of Blues

④ Royale

Housed in an ornate, bi-level theater, the Royale *(see p111)* can accommodate more nightlife deni-zens than any other Boston club. Top 40, 1980s, Latin, and house music

Lauryn Hill performing at Royale

are pumped through the powerful sound system, while a mixed crowd lounges around on cushy banquettes or throngs the mammoth dance floor.

5 Blue Hills Bank Pavilion

MAP H4 ■ 290 Northern Ave ■ 617 728 1600

This circular 1-acre (0.4 ha) outdoor amphitheater, originally known as Harbor Lights, is one of Boston's prime summer concert venues. It seats more than 5,000 spectators beneath a grand tent that shields them from inclement weather. Cool harbor breezes and state-of-the-art lighting and sound systems enhance the experience.

6 Brighton Music Hall

MAP A4 ■ 158 Brighton Ave ■ 617 779 0140 ■ Adm

Set in the heart of Allston, Brighton Music Hall is a premiere live performance venue and primarily caters to college and university students. The 400-capacity concert hall hosts up-and-coming national and local rock, pop, alternative, and indie rock bands as well as stand-up comedy shows.

7 Whisky Saigon

The sumptuous, dark interior, glam lighting, and extensive range of designer vodkas combine a stylish high-tech approach with enchanting, old-fashioned romanticism. It is easy to see why this attention-seekers' paradise has topped various polls, including sexiest bar and best pick-up spot (see p111).

8 Orpheum Theatre

MAP G4 ■ 1 Hamilton Pl ■ 617 482 0106 ■ Adm

Boston's oldest music venue, the Orpheum dates from 1852. After serving as a vaudeville house and a movie theater, it has now become a beloved venue for touring rock bands and comedy concerts.

9 Paradise Rock Club

MAP C5 ■ 967 Commonwealth Ave ■ 617 562 8800 ■ Adm

Although no longer in its original Downtown location, the Paradise is the oldest name in Boston rock venues. Icons from the 1970s and 1980s such as Van Halen, the Police, and Blondie first put the club on the map. Today, the Paradise remains true to its rock 'n' roll roots, welcoming nationally recognized acts that favor volume levels north of ten.

Performers at Scullers Jazz Club

10 Scullers Jazz Club

MAP C4 ■ 400 Soldiers Field Rd ■ 617 562 4111 ■ Closed Sun ■ Adm

Enthusiastic champion of Latin jazz and emerging artists (for example, Norah Jones and Diana Krall started here), Scullers is also a well-known venue for internationally established musicians. It's a great place to enjoy a drink and an evening of smooth jazz by some of the best performers in the business.

TOP 10 Gay and Lesbian Hangouts

Classy interior of Club Café

1 Club Café
MAP M6 ■ 209 Columbus Ave

A video lounge and a popular Sunday brunch infallibly bring out the beautiful boys at this multifunctional South End meeting spot with great bar staff. Find a seat in the casually elegant restaurant, which puts inspired twists on classic continental fare, the mirrored bar area – perfect for scoping the room – or the sleek cocktail lounge out the back.

2 Midway Café
3496 Washington St, Jamaica Plain ■ Adm

Having offered its stage to rockabilly, punk, swing, reggae, and hip-hop acts since 1987, the Midway Café is partially responsible for Jamaica Plain's (see p132) youth-driven renaissance. Most nights bring an eclectic, edgy mix of music lovers, both gay and straight. The club's Thursday Queeraoke Night is one of the most popular lesbian club night in town.

3 dbar
This popular Dorchester spot has a split personality: trendy, full-service neighborhood bistro by day, popular gay dance club at night. "Show Tunes Tuesdays" are a wildly popular sing-along that can get a bit rowdy late in the evening.

The decor features lots of warm wood and brass that creates an inviting atmosphere (see p134).

4 Diesel Café
257 Elm St, Somerville

This hipster-filled coffee shop, in the heart of Somerville's bustling Davis Square, is a favorite hangout among the area's young gay and lesbian couples. The varied menu runs the gamut from gourmet coffee drinks and inventive tea concoctions to tasty snacks. Its spacious, relaxed vibe is great for chatting an afternoon away.

5 Machine
MAP E5 ■ 1254 Boylston St ■ Adm

A recent facelift saw Machine absorb the dated, hardcore Ramrod that used to be in the same building. Machine is now a two-story, mostly gay nightclub, that also attracts a growing straight audience with themed nights, including drag shows, karaoke, and a busy dance floor packed (particularly on weekends) with mostly young, beautiful bodies. Male go-go dancers and DJ-led dance nights featuring the best dance music of the 1980s, 1990s, and 2000s help round out the offerings.

Popular nightclub Machine

6 Guerilla Queer Bar
www.thewelcomingcommittee.com/boston#boston-takeovers

This is not a place, but a viral event. On the first Friday of each month scores, and sometimes hundreds, of LGBTQ partygoers descend on an otherwise vanilla-straight bar or nightclub. The result is fun and uplifting for everyone – so much so that it is becoming a nationwide phenomenon. Check the website for the forthcoming venue.

7 The Alley Bar
MAP P3 ■ 275 Washington St ■ 617 263 1449

The Alley has a mellow, sociable vibe, with activities including karaoke, pool tournaments, underwear parties, and other theme nights for men who want to meet men. A big Alley attraction is the Saturday-night Bear Party for full-framed guys and those who love them. There is an upstairs/downstairs set-up which separates the various theme-night crowds from local drinkers.

8 Paradise Bar
MAP D3 ■ 180 Massachusetts Ave, Cambridge ■ 617 868 3000

This Central Square club is best known for having live performances by male dancers six nights a week, and for fielding new amateur talent. The upstairs bar shows big-screen movies and concert videos, while downstairs is a dance hall (no high heels are allowed).

9 Jacque's Cabaret
One of the oldest names on the Boston gay club scene, Jacque's has been welcoming queer rock bands, drag queens, and their adoring fans for many decades. Garage rock and beer fuel the crowded area around

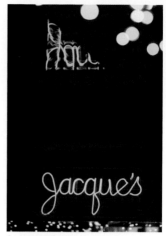

Jacque's Cabaret

the popular pool tables. Discreetly tucked away behind the Theater District, Jacque's is a lively option every night of the week (see p111).

10 Boston Eagle
MAP F6 ■ 520 Tremont St

A doorway-mounted wooden eagle has welcomed gay men to this subterranean South End bar for years. Having no qualms about simply being a gay bar, the Eagle is not a place to dance. The dimly lit bar area is roomy and comfortable; in the back, a mirrored wall captures pool sharks and pinball wizards at work.

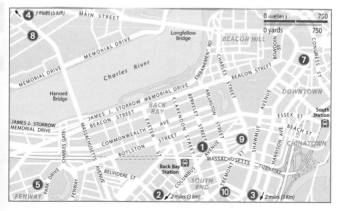

Bars

1 Drink
MAP R5 ■ 348 Congress St
■ 617 695 1806

This trendy subterranean bar in the Fort Point district wins praise for its impressive lineup of classic and classically inspired cocktails. Knowledgeable bartenders may quiz you to create a drink to suit your character. The house signature drink here is the Fort Point variation on a Manhattan.

2 Haley.Henry Wine Bar
A local favorite, Haley.Henry is a small, stylish wine bar *(see p104)* located in the heart of Downtown Crossing. Known for its thoughtfully curated wine list, which is available by the glass as well as by the half-bottle, the bar also serves beer. The menu features cheese and charcuterie boards, crudo, and imported varieties of tinned fish.

3 Oak Long Bar & Kitchen
The Copley Plaza hotel bar *(see p92)* serves a full roster of craft cocktails and a farm-to-table seasonal dining menu. In summer, drinks and meals can be enjoyed on the outdoor patio, which appropriately enough overlooks the twice-weekly farmers' market.

4 Delux Café
The kind of place that is so special, you want to keep it a secret. The South End's intimate Delux Café *(see p111)* attracts a refreshing mix of professionals, bike messengers, and gay boys and girls – all suckers for the bar's kitschy Elvis motif, extensive on-tap beers, and constant broadcast of the Cartoon Network.

5 Bar at the Taj
Originally the cigar lounge of Boston's first luxury hotel, the Bar at the Taj *(see p92)* is a great place for sipping a dram of Scotch by a fireplace or enjoying craft cocktails that are bound to become new classics. The refreshing Three G, for example, blends the Taj's own gin, St Germain, grapefruit juice, and orange bitters.

6 Les Zygomates
The dinner crowd at Les Zygomates (the French term for the facial muscles that make you smile) is lured by reasonably priced French bistro fare. After 9pm, the sleek, whimsically designed bar in the restaurant *(see p113)* comes alive with young professionals enjoying the nightly live jazz performances.

Plush interior of Oak Long Bar & Kitchen

Jazz musicians at Regattabar

7 Regattabar

The giants of jazz often stop at this nautical-themed lounge *(see p128)* in Cambridge's Charles Hotel. Drinks may not be extraordinary but the talent is; past visitors have included McCoy Tyner, Ron Carter, and local favorite the Charlie Kolhase Quintet. Shows sell out quickly so buy tickets in advance.

8 Hawthorne

This suave craft cocktail bar anchors the nightlife scene at the Hotel Commonwealth in Kenmore Square. Lounge-like in the front, cozy in the back, it's the place to drink and socialize *(see p120)*. Creative house cocktails, and the first-rate wine list includes several sparkling wines by the glass.

9 City Winery

Located close to TD Garden, this relaxed wine bar and restaurant *(see p85)* has a well-designed performance space that hosts live music concerts as well as stand-up comedy shows. There's also a winery on site that conducts tours and tastings, and is a perfect place to sample different wines on tap.

10 Alibi

Set in the former drunk tank of the Charles Street Jail (now the posh Liberty Hotel), Alibi *(see p85)* retains the bluestone floors and vestiges of the cell walls to form little nooks to lounge in while enjoying a drink or two. The outdoor patio is great for cocktails at sunset. There's also an upscale Italian restaurant on site.

TOP 10 LOCALLY BREWED BEERS

1 Night Shift Awake
Porter aged with coffee picks you up and puts you down.

2 Harpoon IPA
Ranked among the top domestic and imported India pale ales by *Beer Connoisseur Magazine*.

3 John Harvard's Nut Brown
Try this malty, light ale served at John Harvard's Brew House (33 Dunster St, Cambridge).

4 Clown Shoes Hoppy Feet
Grapefruit and pine on the nose, with dark chocolate and nuts on the palate.

5 Boston Beer Works Fenway Pale Ale
Don your Red Sox cap and sip a light Fenway Pale at Boston Beer Works *(see p120)*.

6 Samuel Adams Boston Lager
The beer that put Sam back on the brewing map after a 200-year hiatus.

7 Lamplighter Metric Systems
Only at Cambridge taproom, this lemon-tangy Gose wheat beer is a brewery signature.

8 Samuel Adams Cherry Wheat Ale
Like a hybrid between champagne and cherry soda; available at most liquor stores.

9 Harpoon UFO Hefeweizen
Unfiltered, Belgian-style brew, with fruity undertones.

10 Samuel Adams Octoberfest
Sam's finest – available only during the autumn – with deep amber coloring and a warm, spicy smoothness.

Samuel Adams Octoberfest mugs

🔟 Restaurants

1 L'Espalier

Adjoining the luxury Mandarin Oriental hotel *(see p146)*, in the heart of fashionable Back Bay, this is one of Boston's top restaurants *(see p93)*. The award-winning, modern French cuisine emphasizes local ingredients in dishes such as butter-poached Maine lobster and cocoa-rubbed venison. Only expensive fixed-price and tasting menus are offered during dinner service.

Elegant L'Espalier

2 Uni

Local culinary titan Ken Oringer and chef-partner Tony Messina operate this lively, upscale izakaya *(see p93)* in the ground level of Back Bay's Eliot Hotel. Small plates of global street foods dot the menu, along with fresh takes on makimoni, nigri, and sashimi. Cult ramen meals are served late on weekend nights.

3 Mamma Maria

This upscale eatery *(see p99)* is located in a 19th-century row house and is loaded with old-world charm. Its daily changing menu specializes in classic Italian comfort cuisine with a twist. For example, the clam pasta features not only famous Falmouth (Cape Cod) clams, but also toasted pine nuts, prosciutto, and sautéd green pea tendrils. Save room for the excellent dessert list, which features highlights such as Nonna's chocolate torte with creamy espresso gelato.

Uni's tuna sashimi

4 Grill 23 & Bar

Easily Boston's finest steakhouse, Grill 23 *(see p93)* features one of the city's best wine lists and a number of delicious alternatives to seared slabs of perfect beef. Swordfish, sea bass, salmon, and lobster satisfy the pescatarians. Sides include lobster mac and cheese with smoked Gouda, and fries with a house harissa ketchup.

5 Trade

Trade is the fine-dining anchor to the Greenway Park that links Downtown and the waterfront. Set in the Atlantic Wharf building, it makes use of Mediterranean flavors while remaining true to its New England roots. Both ends of that historic trade route shine in dishes such as braised short rib with Jerusalem artichoke, olives and orange. The restaurant *(see p99)* is popular for its light lunches, which feature freshly made sandwiches and salads.

6 Toro

Chef-owners Ken Oringer and Jamie Bissonnette team up for one of the city's hardest-to-get-into restaurants *(see p111)*. This South End hot spot serves a mix of modern and traditional tapas, paella, refreshing cocktails, and Spanish wines. Head here for excellent Latin food served in stylish environs, from a menu filled with trendy imported items as well as a host of original dishes. The special Sunday brunch is popular.

Menton's exquisite cuisine

7 Menton

Superchef Barbara Lynch's elegant Fort Point dining room (see p99) regularly receives national-level rave reviews for its dishes. Diners can choose from one of two tasting menus, with offerings such as lobster and chamomile with fava, hazelnut, and Meyer lemon; or tart of foie gras enhanced with wild ramps, beetroot, and spring onion. All diners at a table are requested to choose the same menu.

8 Craigie On Main

Award-winning chef Tony Maws, acclaimed for his French-inspired nose-to-tail approach to fine dining, presides over a bustling open kitchen facing the dining area, filled with an eclectic mix of diners. The menu here (see p129) changes daily, based on the locally sourced organic ingredients picked up at the market that morning. Head to the bar for the wildly popular gourmet burger, served with big, chunky fries, and great cocktails.

9 Meritage

Chef Daniel Bruce showcases perfect pairings of food and wine at this elegant eatery in the Boston Harbor Hotel. Diners choose dishes from either a red/rosé wine menu or a white/sparkling wine menu, as part of his innovative vineyard-to-table philosophy. The restaurant (see p99) hosts the famous Boston Wine Festival in January.

10 Harvest

Since the 1970s, this relaxed restaurant (see p129) has been a leader in setting the direction of American cuisine. Chef Tyler Kinnet brings a Mediterranean palate to New England cuisine, pairing lobster with favas and nasturtium blossoms or roasting pork with local fennel, garlic, and stone fruits. The outdoor garden terrace is lovely.

Bar at Harvest

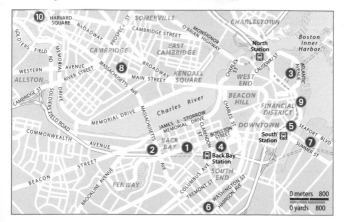

TOP 10 Spots for Seafood

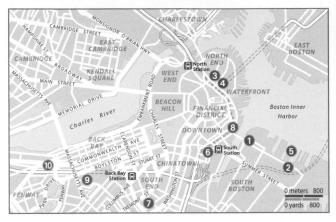

1 Barking Crab
MAP H4 ▪ 88 Sleeper St
▪ 617 426 2722 ▪ $$$

This colorful fish shack is most congenial in the summer, when diners sit outdoors at picnic tables, but there's also indoor seating with a cozy wood-burner for chillier days. Most of the local fish – cod, haddock, tuna, halibut, clams, and crab – are so fresh that they need only the most simple preparation.

2 Legal Harborside

The Seaport flagship (see p99) of the Legal Sea Foods chain makes dockside dining chic. You'll find a no-frills, casual dining room, oyster bar, and a traditional fish market on level one; there's fine dining featuring beautifully prepared fish on level two; while level three offers a four-season rooftop lounge and bar, with retractable glass roof and walls, serving ocean-fresh sushi and cocktails. All three spaces come with a stunning harbor view.

Dish at Legal Harborside

3 Neptune Oyster

Exceptionally fresh choices from the raw bar vie for attention with dishes from the expertly prepared dinner menu. Choose an old favorite, such as clam chowder, or a more daring dish like Spanish octopus with hazelnut romesco. The simple dining room of this restaurant (see p99) ensures that the food is the focus of attention. Reservations are not accepted so arrive early and be prepared to wait for a table – it's worth it.

4 Mare Oyster Bar
MAP H3 ▪ 3 Mechanic St
▪ 617 723 6273
▪ Closed L Mon
▪ $$$

Mare specializes in Italian coastal cuisine. Begin with the raw bar or a trio of crudos, then savor a classic seafood pasta dish or grilled fish – or indulge yourself with a decadent lobster roll on brioche, along with a plate of fries. A few meat dishes are also available. To accompany your meal, enjoy a cocktail or glass of wine from their enticing drinks menu.

5 No Name Restaurant
15½ Fish Pier ■ 617 423 2705
■ $

Fish Pier's only restaurant has an intimate relationship with the fishermen who both sell their catch to, and eat at, this bare-bones place. The very basic menu consists mostly of fried fish, while the great chowder is full of what fishermen call "trim" – chunks of whatever has been caught, boned and trimmed that day.

6 O Ya
Combining Japanese tradition and American invention, this elegant restaurant (see p105) proves that good things come in small packages. Offering both sweet and savoury dishes, half the menu is sushi and sashimi, and the other half meat and vegetarian. With six chefs at work, each bite-sized portion is exquisitely executed. Ask for the *omakase* (tasting) menu and let the excellent head chef Tim Cushman wow you with a culinary *tour de force*.

B&G Oysters

7 B&G Oysters
MAP F6 ■ 550 Tremont St
■ 617 423 0550 ■ $$$

This brightly lit underground seafood spot is both oyster bar – there are a dozen varieties ready to be shucked at any moment – and seafood bistro.

8 James Hook & Co.
MAP H5 ■ 15 Northern Ave
■ 617 423 5500 ■ Closed evenings ■ $

A family-owned business located right on Fort Point Channel, Hook is primarily a broker that supplies lobster to restaurants throughout

Exterior of James Hook & Co.

the US. However, they also cook lobster, clams, crab, and some fin fish on the spot. Take your order, sit on the sea wall, and chow down. Many visitors find it the best place to eat good, reasonably priced seafood.

9 Summer Shack
MAP K6 ■ 50 Dalton St ■ 617 867 9955 ■ Closed L Mon–Fri Nov–Mar ■ $$

Boston celebrity chef Jasper White literally wrote the book on lobster, but he's just as adept with wood-grilled fresh fish and delicate fried shellfish. A fabulous raw bar and colorful summer fish-shack atmosphere match well with the extensive beer list. It's a great place to bring kids who like to crack their own crabs.

10 Island Creek Oyster Bar
MAP D5 ■ 500 Commonwealth Ave ■ 617 532 5300 ■ Closed L Mon–Sat ■ $$$

Partly owned by the Duxbury oyster farm of the same name, this upscale yet casual restaurant excels at shellfish (including eight varieties of New England oysters) and does great things with fin fish, too. Their seafood casserole brings together shrimp, lobster, clams, scallops, and cod in a single delectable bowl.

Lobster at Island Creek Oyster Bar

For a key to restaurant price ranges see p85

📕🔟 Cafés

Comfortable split-level interior of Thinking Cup

1 Thinking Cup
MAP G4 ■ 165 Tremont St

A cozy place to socialize on Boston Common, Thinking Cup serves teas and Stumptown-roasted coffee. Knowledgeable baristas offer assistance with your choice of espresso drinks or pour-overs. The menu also includes tempting pastries and sandwiches.

2 Wired Puppy
MAP K5 ■ 250 Newbury St

This coffee shop in the middle of Newbury Street is popular with the local office crowd. Try their artisan espresso, gourmet coffee drinks, and fresh pastries. There's also free use of their computer and Wi-Fi.

3 Caffè Vittoria
MAP Q1 ■ 296 Hanover St

The jukebox at the largest of North End's Italian cafés is heavily loaded with songs recorded by Frank Sinatra, Tony Bennett, and Al Martino. The menu is long on short coffees and short drinks, including at least seven varieties of grappa, as well as a fair selection of Italian ices.

4 Mike's Pastry

Mike's is legendary for its 20 or so flavors of fresh cannolis. There is a café where all the baked goodies are available – cupcakes, biscotti, brownies, cakes, pies, cookies, and specialty items – along with gourmet brews. The lines can be long, especially on weekends, but they do tend to move quickly *(see p98).*

5 Sonsie
MAP J6 ■ 327 Newbury St

Although continental breakfast is served, Sonsie doesn't really get going until lunchtime. By dusk, it is full of folks who just stopped in for a post-work drink and ended up making an evening of it. The food – pizza, pasta, and fusion-tinged entrées – deserves more attention than most café-goers give it.

6 Barrington Coffee Roasting Company Café
MAP H5 ■ 346 Congress St, Fort Point

This western Massachusetts coffee roaster brought its acclaimed selection of single-origin coffees to this artistic neighborhood at Fort Point Channel. There is a second outlet now at Newbury Street. Espresso and drip coffee get equal billing, as many of the lighter roasts are best brewed one drip cup at a time. Regular tasting events are a popular feature.

7 1369 Coffee House

A community-based café, 1369 has a definite neighborly atmosphere. The original Inman Square branch *(see p127)* has a more interesting cross section of ages and ethnicities but Central Square has sidewalk seating.

Both branches serve mostly caffeine drinks and sweets – with sandwiches at lunch.

8 Dado Tea

However you like your tea – white, black, or green – this eco-friendly shop serves a choice of blends, alongside organic wraps, sandwiches and salads. Dado offers a selection of gluten-free and vegan options too. Coffee-lovers are accommodated, but tea rules here *(see p127)*.

9 Blue State Coffee
MAP H4 ■ 155 Seaport Blvd

This community-oriented coffee shop serves a variety of freshly roasted fair trade coffee. The menu features salads, sandwiches, and granola, all made with locally sourced produce. The café also sells savory and sweet scones, muffins and cakes, including vegan and gluten-free options. Blue State donates a percentage of their sales to local non-profit organizations.

10 Max Brenner
MAP E4 ■ 745 Boylston St

Chocoholics will demand a trip to this celebration of all things cocoa. Savor a chocolate martini, or try the Illegal Chocolate Chocolate Chocolate Pancakes, made with 70 percent dark chocolate cream, milk chocolate shavings, spiced pecans and caramelized bananas. There are non-chocolate dishes too, such as smoked mozzarella and mushroom mac and cheese.

Max Brenner's chocolate café

TOP 10 SPOTS TO BREAK YOUR DIET

L. A. Burdick Chocolatiers

1 L. A. Burdick Chocolatiers
MAP B1 ■ 52D Brattle St, Cambridge
Boston's best hot chocolate accompanied by sinful bonbons.

2 Swissbäkers
168 Western Ave, Allston
Family-run company producing delicious European pastries.

3 Union Square Donuts
20 Bow St, Somerville
Small batches of donuts in sweet and savory flavors.

4 La Sultana Bakery
240 Maverick Sq, East Boston
French and Columbian delicacies.

5 Flour Bakery & Café
MAP F6; 1595 Washington St
■ MAP R5; 12 Farnsworth St
Delicious cakes, cookies, and cups of excellent coffee.

6 Lulu's Sweet Shoppe
MAP H3 ■ 28 Parmenter St
Lulu's specializes in gourmet cupcakes and retro candies.

7 Eldo Cake House
MAP P4 ■ 36 Harrison Ave
Tucked away in Chinatown, Eldo has Western-style iced cakes and Chinese treats.

8 Lizzy's Ice Cream
MAP B1 ■ 29 Church St, Cambridge
Chopped candy bars and sundae toppings in super-rich ice cream.

9 Langham Boston Chocolate Bar
MAP Q4 ■ 250 Franklin St ■ Open Sep–Jun: Sat
A delicious range of French chocolate pastry and sweets.

10 Christina's Homemade Ice Cream
MAP D2 ■ 1255 Cambridge St, Cambridge
Exotic spices and flavors add punch.

TOP 10 Essential Shopping Experiences

Exterior of Boston Public Market

1 Boston Public Market
MAP Q2 ■ 100 Hanover St

Modern public market features around 40 farmers, fishers, and other small food producers in bright setting. The many vendors of prepared food make it a good breakfast or lunch option. A demo kitchen hosts various activities.

2 Garment District
MAP D2 ■ 200 Broadway, Cambridge

The vintage clothing and bargain-priced trends of the Garment District are every Boston hipster's retort to fashion. Fancy-dress costumes are found on the first floor, but you can also find retro goods, office wear, and even clothing sold by the pound.

3 Artists' Open Studios
www.boston.gov

Boston's visual artists open their studios to the public on selected spring and fall weekends. Boston's numerous studio events are mostly in converted former warehouses. One of the most popular is the South End Open Studio event. Start at the Boston Center for the Arts (see p54), where there are many studios nearby, and pick up a map for the rest.

4 Copley Place
MAP L6 ■ 100 Huntington Ave

This was among the country's first upscale urban shopping malls. It counts high-end stores such as Louis Vuitton, Tiffany, Neiman Marcus, and Coach as its tenants. Footwear addicts are fond of Stuart Weitzman and Jimmy Choo boutiques.

5 Red Sox Team Store
MAP D5 ■ 19 Jersey St

With World Series titles dating back to 1903 and the oldest ballpark in professional baseball, the Boston Red Sox engender a fan loyalty matched by few other teams. This memorabilia shop, across the street from Fenway Park (see p117), sells every permutation of hat, jersey, and T-shirt imaginable, as well as signed bats, balls, and gloves, and baseball cards for hardcore collectors.

Red Sox merchandise

6 Newbury Street

Try as it might, Back Bay's most famous street cannot escape its regional reputation as the city's Beverly Hills' Rodeo Drive. True, both offer stupendous people-watching, sophisticated shopping, chic dining, and prestigious galleries. Yet, with its 19th-century charm and convenient subway stops, Newbury Street outclasses its built-yesterday Left Coast counterpart by far (see pp24–5).

7 Harvard Square Bookstores

MAP B1

Harvard Square's bookstores are some of the country's most distinguished. The Harvard Coop carries 170,000-plus titles, while rival Harvard Book Store (1256 Massachusetts Ave) stocks countless new and used books and hosts readings. Nearby Grolier Poetry Bookshop (6 Plympton St) is verse central, while Raven Used Books (23 Church St) stocks 15,000 academic and literary titles.

The Harvard Coop bookstore

8 Charles Street

MAP M3

This charming, bluest-of-blue-blooded street is studded with antique dealers *(see p84)*, specialty grocers, and modern houseware boutiques. Come nightfall, wrought-iron gas lamps illuminate the brick sidewalks, residents hurry home with wine and fresh flowers, and sleek bistros buzz with excitement.

Georgian-style facade of Faneuil Hall

9 Faneuil Hall Marketplace

With its millions of visitors each year, Faneuil Hall Marketplace would not be found on any best-kept secret list. However, its central location, rich colonial history, and plethora of food stalls mean that it offers a unique retail experience. Shoppers can choose from name-brand stores such as Victoria's Secret or the more unusual offerings from New England artisans *(see p101)*.

10 SoWa Open Market

MAP G6 ■ 460 Harrison Ave

Expect a wide range of clothing, jewelry, and art at Boston's art and indie design market, held every Sunday in the South End. A farmers' market augments the summer scene as top Boston food trucks feed hungry shoppers.

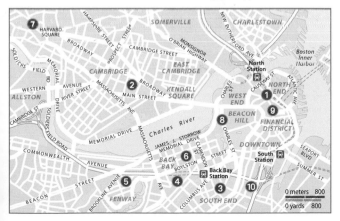

TOP 10 Boston for Free

USS *Constitution* or "Old Ironsides"

1 Charlestown Navy Yard

The Charlestown Navy Yard is home to the USS *Constitution*, the famous Revolutionary War-era frigate known as "Old Ironsides". Also here is the 1943 destroyer USS *Cassin Young*. Both admission and the ranger-led tours of the ships are free *(see pp36–7)*.

2 Hatch Shell

Fridays from June through August are free, family movie nights at the Hatch Shell, located on the banks of the Charles River. The Hatch Shell *(see p54)* also hosts free concerts throughout the year, including Boston Pops' Fourth of July concert.

3 Mount Auburn Cemetery

580 Mt Auburn St, Cambridge ▪ 617 547 7105 ▪ www.mountauburn.org
One of the best places to take a walk in the city is historic Mount Auburn Cemetery, which serves as a park, botanical garden and arboretum, as well as the final resting place of luminaries ranging from poet Henry Wadsworth Longfellow to inventor Buckminster Fuller. The stunningly beautiful 0.3-sq-mile- (0.7-sq-km-) grounds feature 3 miles (5 km) of walking trails and miles of quiet roadways.

4 Black Heritage Trail

In the 19th century, Boston's thriving black community was a driving force in the fight to end slavery and, in the 20th century, they strove to achieve equality. A free National Park Service tour of the Black Heritage Trail *(see p82)* visits a diverse range of historic homes, schools, and businesses that tell the story of Boston's early African-American citizens. Included are visits to the first black public school in America and the 1806 African Meeting House.

5 Freedom Trail

One of the most popular activities for visitors in Boston is walking the self-guided Freedom Trail *(see pp12–13)*. Touring the trail is free, as are entering all but four of the 16 sites and attractions along the way. Allow at least half a day for this stroll through history.

Freedom Trail Town Crier

6 Harvard Square

MAP C2 ▪ www.harvard square.com
One of Boston's liveliest public spaces is also a great place for people-watching. There are always buskers performing, and it hosts a regular schedule of events including outdoor musical and theater performances. In September, thousands of locals come to take part in the free, one-night RiverSing to celebrate the fall equinox.

People gathered in Harvard Square

7 Shakespeare on Boston Common

MAP N2 ■ 617 426 0863 ■ www. commshakes.org

The Commonwealth Shakespeare Company performs one of the Bard's plays free-of-charge on Boston Common each July and August. Perfomances are often preceded by free musical concerts.

8 Boston HarborWalk

www.bostonharbornow.org

Connecting public parks, historic sites, and points of interest from Charlestown to South Boston, HarborWalk is an ideal place for cycling or walking. When completed it will stretch 43 miles (69 km).

Stretch of Boston HarborWalk

9 Fort Independence

Fort Independence on Castle Island (see p46), at the entrance to Boston's inner harbor, was a cutting-edge military defence system when it was begun in 1834. Free tours are available in summer. Be sure to stop at Sullivan's legendary hot-dog stand, which is found nearby.

10 Free Guided Tours

There are many free guided tours available around Boston. Four of the most popular are the Freedom Trail (see pp12–13), Faneuil Hall (see p101), the Boston Public Library (see p87), and the Samuel Adams Brewery (see p51). Other options include Harvard Yard (see pp20–21) and the Massachusetts State House (see p15).

MONEY SAVING TIPS

BosTix ticket booth

1 Bargain Tickets
www.artsboston.org
BosTix kiosks sell discounted tickets to many events on performance day.

2 CityPass
www.citypass.com
A CityPass ($59) gives discounted access to many sights.

3 Go Boston Card
www.smartdestinations.com
Save up to 55 percent on entry to a wide range of sights with this card.

4 Public Transit Passes
MBTA passes allow unlimited travel on subways, buses, and ferries (see p138).

5 Museum Admission
Some Boston museums, such as the Museum of Fine Arts, offer free or pay-what-you-want admission.

6 Special Discounts
Student and senior citizen discounts are often available with identification.

7 College Galleries
College and university art galleries offer some of the city's most provocative exhibitions, with free admission.

8 Boston Symphony Savings
Reduced-price tickets for rehearsals and for people under age 40 are available at Symphony Hall (see p54).

9 Theater Deals
www.huntingtontheatre.org
The Huntington Theatre has $30 tickets for under-35s; as well as a limited number of $25 tickets for all ages at every performance.

10 Music Schools
Berklee Performance Center (see p55) offers discounted performances. The New England Conservatory holds free performances at Jordan Hall (see p55).

TOP 10 Festivals and Events

Dancers celebrating the Chinese New Year

Chinese New Year
Jan/ Feb

Chinatown *(see pp106–113)* buzzes with the pageantry of the Chinese New Year. Streets are transformed into patchworks of color, while sidewalk vendors peddle steamed buns, soups, and other Chinese delights. Don't miss the annual parade, held the Saturday following the Lunar New Year.

2 Boston Flower and Garden Show
A week in mid-Mar ■ www.boston flowershow.com

Over 150,000 visitors descend on this indoor exhibition, hosted at the Seaport World Trade Center, to forget their winter blues and enjoy the spectacular display of bright blooms and fragrant aromas.

3 St. Patrick's Day
Mid-Mar

Boston's immense Irish-American population explains why few, if any, American cities can match Boston's Irish pride. Come Paddy's Day, pubs host live Irish bands and increasingly raucous crowds as the Guinness and the Shamrock-green ale flow freely. The weekend South Boston Parade, with its famous drum corps, starts off from Broadway "T" station.

4 Dine Out Boston
Mar & Aug ■ www. bostonusa.com/dine-out-boston

For two weeks in March and August, more than 100 restaurants in Boston, Cambridge, and neighboring suburbs offer bargain, fixed-price lunch and dinner menus. Locals look forward to, and make the most of, the opportunity to sample new restaurants, so it is wise to make reservations.

5 Lilac Sunday
2nd Sun in May ■ www. arboretum.harvard.edu

While the Arnold Arboretum *(see p131)* includes 4,463 species of flora, one plant deserves particular celebration. When its 500 lilac plants are at their fragrant, color-washed peak, garden enthusiasts arrive in droves for picnics, music, and walking tours of the lilac collections.

6 Boston Calling
Late May ■ www.boston calling.com

National headliners and new, up-and-coming acts perform live, with non-stop music for three days in late May at the Harvard Athletic Complex, to sell-out crowds. It's a family-friendly festival, with three stages and a good variety of high-energy performers and musical styles. In recent years, Boston Calling has featured the likes of Beck, the Pixies, Kendrick Lamar, Lorde, and the Alabama Shakes.

7 Cambridge Arts River Festival
Early Jun ■ www.cambridgema. gov/arts/Programs/riverfestival

On a Saturday in early June the banks of the Charles River in

Cambridge host a celebration of the city's lively and diverse population. Musicians and dancers perform and artists sell their wares. Food vendors offer a taste of home.

8 Fourth of July
Jul 4

Given Boston's crucial role in securing independence for the original 13 colonies, Independence Day adopts a certain importance here. With parties, barbecues and a fireworks display on the Charles River banks, Boston throws the nation a spectacular birthday party.

Boston Pops' Fourth of July concert

9 Feast of St. Anthony
Last weekend in Aug

The Feast of St. Anthony caps an entire summer of feast holidays in the North End (see pp94–9). From morning through well into the night, Hanover Street bulges with revelers, parades, and food vendors giving a vibrant display of the area's old-world Italian spirit.

10 First Night
Dec 31

Despite the possibility of staggeringly cold weather, the New Year's Eve festivities remain among the most highly anticipated events of Boston's year. Free and open to all, the events are usually held around Copley Square and Back Bay. They include a parade, beautifully lit ice sculptures, light displays, and family-friendly fireworks at 7pm on the Common.

TOP 10 SPORTING TRADITIONS

Boston Celtics in action

1 Boston Celtics
617 624 1000
The Celts keep basketball playoff dreams alive at the TD Garden.

2 Head of the Charles Regatta
3rd Sat & Sun Oct ▪ 617 868 6200
Rowing crews race down the Charles while the banks teem with onlookers.

3 Red Sox vs Yankees
617 267 1700
The most heated rivalry in US sports flares up every time the Yanks visit Fenway Park (see p117).

4 Boston Marathon
3rd Mon Apr ▪ 617 236 1652
The country's oldest marathon.

5 Boston Bruins
617 624 1000
Crowds cheer this ice hockey team at the TD Garden.

6 New England Patriots
800 543 1776
Gillette Stadium is the home of the Patriots, five-time Super Bowl champs.

7 Harvard vs Yale
617 495 3454
These Ivy League football teams butt helmets in Cambridge every other fall.

8 Beanpot Hockey Tournament
617 624 1000
Every February Boston's top collegiate hockey teams play each other.

9 New England Revolution
800 543 1776
The local entry in Major League Soccer is an annual playoff threat at Gillette Stadium.

10 New Year's Day Swim
The "L Street Brownies" swimming club takes a dip in Boston Harbor every January 1.

🔟 Day Trips: Historic New England

1 Lexington

Massachusetts ■ Route 2
■ **Visitor information: 1875 Massachusetts Ave; 1 781 862 1450**
■ **www.lexingtonchamber.org**

Peaceful Lexington Green marks the first encounter of British soldiers with organized resistance by American revolutionaries. The rebels fortified their courage with a night of drinking at the adjacent Buckman Tavern.

Minuteman statue, Lexington Green

2 Concord

Massachusetts ■ Route 2
■ **Visitor information: 58 Main St; 1 978 369 3120 ■ www.concord chamberofcommerce.org**

Rebels put the Redcoats to rout at North Bridge, Concord's main revolutionary battle site. The town was also the hub of American literature in the mid 19th century, and visitors can tour the homes of Ralph Waldo Emerson, Nathaniel Hawthorne, and Louisa May Alcott. Henry David Thoreau's woodland haunts at Walden Pond now feature hiking trails and a swimming beach.

3 New Bedford

Massachusetts ■ Routes I-95 & I-195 ■ Visitor information: 33 William St; 1 508 996 4095
■ **www.nps.gov/nebe**

During the 19th century, local sailors and whalers plundered the oceans of the world, enriching the port of New Bedford. The National Historic District preserves many fine buildings of the era, and the Whaling Museum gives accounts of the enterprise.

4 Plymouth

Massachusetts ■ Routes 3 & 44 ■ Visitor information: 130 Water St; 1 508 747 7525 ■ www. seeplymouth.com

The recreated village of Plimoth Plantation immerses visitors in the lives of the first English settlers in Massachusetts. At the harbor, tour the *Mayflower II* (under renovation through 2019). On Thanksgiving, the town celebrates with a parade in Pilgrim dress.

5 Salem

Massachusetts ■ Route 1A
■ **Visitor information: 2 New Liberty St; 1 978 740 1650 ■ www.nps.gov/sama**

A witch may not have been killed in Salem since 1692, but witchcraft paraphernalia fills many stores, and several sites tell the tale of this dark episode. The city is more proud of its China Trade days (circa 1780–1880), which are engagingly recounted on walking tours. Visit the Peabody Essex Museum to see the treasures sea captains brought home.

Salem Witch Museum

Providence, Rhode Island

⑥ Providence

Rhode Island ■ Routes 1 or I-95 ■ Visitor information: 1 Sabin St; 1 401 751 1177 ■ www.goprovidence.com

Providence is a great walking city. Stroll Benefit Street's "mile of history" to see an impressive group of Colonial and Federal houses, or visit Waterplace Park with its pretty walkways along the Providence River. Atwells Avenue on Federal Hill is Providence's Little Italy, bustling with restaurants and cafés.

⑦ Lowell

Massachusetts ■ Routes I-93, I-95, & 3 ■ Visitor information: 246 Market St; 1 978 970 5000 ■ Adm to Boott Cotton Mills Museum ■ www.nps.gov/lowe

Lowell was the cradle of the US's Industrial Revolution, where entrepreneurs dug power canals and built America's first textile mills on the Merrimack River. The sites within the National Historical Park tell the parallel stories of a wrenching transformation from an agricultural to industrial lifestyle. A 1920s weave room still thunders away at Boott Cotton Mills Museum.

⑧ Old Sturbridge Village

Massachusetts ■ Routes I-90, 20, & 84 ■ Visitor Center: 1 Sturbridge Village Rd; 800 733 1830 ■ www.osv.org

Interpreters in period costume go about their daily lives in a typical 1830s New England village. This large living history museum has more than 40 buildings on 0.3 sq miles (0.8 sq km). Visitors can get a sense of the era at the village common, mill district, and the farm.

⑨ Portsmouth

New Hampshire ■ Routes 1 or I-95 ■ Visitor information: 500 Market St; 1 603 610 5510 ■ www.goportsmouthnh.com

Founded in 1623 as Strawbery Banke, the historic houses on Marcy Street document three centuries of city life from earliest settlement through to 20th-century immigration. Picturesque shops, pubs, and restaurants surround Market Square and line the waterfront, and the surrounding streets house fine examples of Federal architecture.

⑩ Newport

Rhode Island ■ Routes I-93, 24, & 114 ■ Visitor information: 23 America's Cup Ave; 1 401 845 9123 ■ www.discovernewport.org

Newport has been a playground for the rich since the late 1860s. Many of the elaborate "cottages" built by 19th-century industrialists are open for tours, including Breakers on Ochre Point Avenue. For natural beauty, hike the 3.6-mile (5.5-km) Cliff Walk overlooking Narragansett Bay and Easton's Beach.

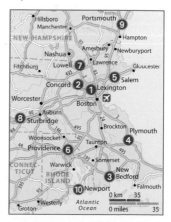

Day Trips: The Beach

1 Cape Ann
Routes I-95 & 127 ▪ **Visitor information: 33 Commercial St, Gloucester; 1 978 283 1601**

Thirty miles (48 km) north of Boston, the granite brow of Cape Ann juts defiantly into the Atlantic – a rugged landscape of precipitous cliffs and deeply cleft harbors. In Gloucester, a waterfront statue and plaque memorialize the 10,000 local fishermen who have perished at sea since 1623, and the Cape Ann Museum displays maritime paintings. The picturesque harborfront of Rockport is an artists' enclave and is lined with galleries.

Sunset at Gloucester, Cape Ann

2 Upper Cape Cod
Routes 3, 6, & 28

The Upper Cape is tranquil and low-key. Visitors can watch the boats glide through Cape Cod Canal or take the Shining Sea bikeway from Falmouth village to Woods Hole. If it's beaches you are after, Sandwich's Sandy Neck has dunes and excellent bird-watching, but Falmouth's Surf Drive is best for swimmers and Old Silver Beach is great for sunset views.

Nantucket Island

3 Mid Cape Cod
Routes 3, 6, & 28

The Mid Cape tends to be congested, especially in the town of Hyannis. But the north shore can be peaceful, with amazing wildlife and stunning views, especially from Gray's Beach in Yarmouth. Warmer water and sandy strands line the south side of Mid Cape, with especially good swimming in Harwich and Dennisport. There's also excellent canoeing and kayaking on the Bass River.

4 Outer Cape Cod
Routes 3 & 6
▪ **www.nps.gov/caco**

Here you'll find some of the area's best beaches. The 40-mile (64-km) National Seashore offers great surfing at Coast Guard and Nauset Light, and the beaches of Marconi, Head of the Meadow, and Race Point all have dramatic dunes and great ocean swimming. The artist colonies of Wellfleet and Truro are worth a visit as is Provincetown, a fishing village turned gay resort.

5 Nantucket Island
Routes 3 & 6 to Hyannis
▪ **Ferry to Nantucket: 1 508 477 1700** ▪ **Visitor information: Zero Main St, Nantucket; 1 508 228 3643; www.nantucketchamber.org**

The Whaling Museum in Nantucket tells the tale of the Quaker whalers who made the island prosperous in the 19th century. It now boasts trophy beach houses and million-dollar yachts. Visitors can enjoy activities such as kayaking, casting

for striped bass from Surfside Beach, or cycling to the village of Sconset with its rose-covered clifftop cottages.

Gay Head Cliffs, Martha's Vineyard

6 Martha's Vineyard
Routes 3 & 28 to Woods Hole ■ Ferry to Vineyard Haven: 1 508 477 8600 ■ Visitor information: 24 Beach St, Vineyard Haven; 1 508 693 0085; www.mvy.com

From Vineyard Haven it's a short drive to Oak Bluffs, with its gingerbread cottages and historic carousel. Venture south to Edgartown and the 19th-century homes of rich whaling captains. Nearby, the 3-mile (5-km) Katama Beach is a magnet for sun worshipers. On the southwest of the island, Menemsha is a picturesque fishing village and Aquinnah's Gay Head Cliffs offer dramatic hiking.

7 Ipswich
Routes 95, 128, & 133, or 1A ■ Visitor information: 36 South Main St; 1 978 356 8540; www.ipswich visitorcenter.org

Crane Beach in Ipswich is one of New England's most scenic, with over 4 miles (6.5 km) of white sand, warm water, and outstanding birdwatching. Also on the Crane Estate, you can visit Castle Hill mansion and its lovely Italianate gardens.

8 Newburyport
Routes I-95 & 1 ■ Visitor information: 38R Merrimac St; 1 978 462 6680

In the 19th century, Newburyport was a prosperous seaport. The grand three-story mansions along the High Street present a virtual case study in Federal architecture, while boutiques and antiques shops line downtown Merrimac, Water, and State streets. The Parker River National Wildlife Refuge on the adjacent Plum Island is one of the US's top bird-watching sanctuaries, with sandpipers, egrets, and piping plovers among its many residents and visitors.

9 Revere Beach
Routes 1 & 1A ■ "T" station: **Revere Beach/Wonderland**

Established in 1896, Revere Beach was the first public beach in the US. Thanks to a centennial restoration, it's also one of the best, with nearly 3 miles (4.5 km) of clean white sand and clear blue water.

10 Hampton & Rye Beaches
Routes I-95, NH 101, & 1A ■ Visitor information: 160 Ocean Blvd, Hampton Bea ch; 1 603 926 8717; www.hamptonbeach.org

The New Hampshire coast just south of Portsmouth has extensive sandy beaches. Wallis Sands State Park is ideal for swimming but the best of the rocky overlooks is Rye's Ragged Neck Point picnic area. The social scene is at Hampton Beach. Odiorne Point State Park in Rye has picnic areas and walking trails.

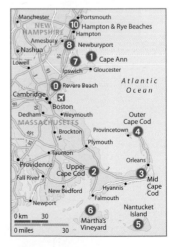

Boston
Area by Area

**Brick-built row houses in
Boston's historic North End**

Beacon Hill	**80**	Chinatown, the Theater District, and South End	**106**
Back Bay	**86**	Kenmore and the Fenway	**116**
North End and the Waterfront	**94**	Cambridge and Somerville	**122**
Downtown and the Financial District	**100**	South of Boston	**130**

TOP 10 Beacon Hill

With its elegant, 19th-century row houses, quaint grocers, pricey antiques shops, and hidden gardens, Beacon Hill screams "old money" like no other area in Boston. The most exclusive block in the district is the genteel Louisburg Square, which was modeled after the Georgian residential squares of London. Throughout the 19th century and well into the 20th, the charming Beacon Hill was

Nichols House Museum exhibit

Louisburg Square on Beacon Hill

a veritable checkerboard of ethnicities and wealth – segregated though they were. Little of Beacon Hill's diversity has survived its inevitable gentrification, but visitors can still experience the neighborhood's myriad pasts inside its opulent mansions and humble schoolhouses, and along its enchanting cobblestone streets.

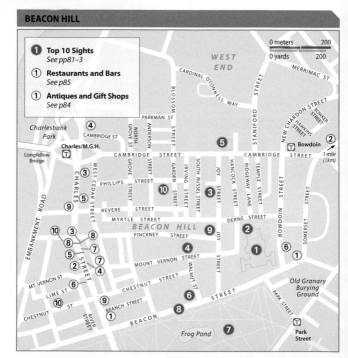

BEACON HILL

① **Top 10 Sights**
See pp81–3

① **Restaurants and Bars**
See p85

① **Antiques and Gift Shops**
See p84

Gleaming dome and elegant frontage of the Massachusetts State House

1 Massachusetts State House

MAP P3 ■ 24 Beacon St ■ 617 727 3676 ■ Tours 10am–3:30pm Mon–Fri (reservations recommended) ■ www.sec.state.ma.us/trs

A 200-year-old codfish, a stained-glass image of a Native American in a grass skirt, and a 23-carat gold dome crowned with a pine cone – these are the curious eccentricities that distinguish Beacon Hill's most prestigious address (see p15).

2 Freedom Trail

MAP P4

Established in the 1950s to provide visitors with a connect-the-dots guide to Boston's colonial-era sites, the Freedom Trail (see pp12–13) runs from Beacon Hill through Downtown, into the North End, and across the Charles River to Charlestown, the site of the famous warship USS Constitution and the Bunker Hill Monument.

3 Museum of African American History

MAP N2 ■ 46 Joy St ■ 617 725 0022 ■ Open 10am–4pm Mon–Sat ■ Adm ■ www.maah.org

Based in the African Meeting House (the oldest extant black church in the US) and the adjoining Abiel Smith School (the nation's first publicly funded grammar school for African-American children), the MAAH offers a look into the daily life of free, pre-Civil War African-Americans. The meeting house was a political and religious center for Boston's African-American community and it was here that abolitionists such as Frederick Douglass and William Lloyd Garrison delivered anti-slavery addresses in the mid-19th century. The museum has successfully preserved their legacy and that of countless others through its wide and fascinating range of workshops, exhibitions, and special events.

4 Nichols House Museum

MAP N3 ■ 55 Mount Vernon St ■ 617 227 6993 ■ Open Apr–Oct: 11am–4pm Tue–Sat; Nov–Mar: 11am–4pm Thu–Sat ■ Adm ■ www.nichols housemuseum.org

An 1804 Charles Bulfinch design, 55 Mount Vernon is one of the earliest examples of residential architecture on Beacon Hill. Rose Nichols, the house's principal occupant for 75 years, bequeathed her home to the city as a museum, providing a glimpse of late 19th- and early 20th-century life on the Hill. A pioneering force for women in the arts and sciences, Nichols gained fame through her authoritative writings on landscape architecture and philanthropic projects.

Skaters enjoying the Frog Pond on Boston Common

5 Harrison Gray Otis House

MAP N2 ■ 141 Cambridge St
■ 617 994 5920 ■ Open Apr–Nov:
11am–4:30pm Wed–Sun ■ Adm
■ www.historicnewengland.org

One of the principal developers of
Beacon Hill, Harrison Gray Otis *(see
p44)*, served in the Massachusetts
legislature and gained a reputation
for living the high life in this 1796
Bulfinch-designed manse. Like a post-
revolutionary Gatsby, Otis ensured
his parties were the social events of
the year. After falling into disrepair, the
property was acquired in 1916 by the
historical preservation society and has
been restored to its original grandeur.

6 Parkman House

MAP N3 ■ 33 Beacon St
■ Closed to the public

George Parkman – once a prominent
physician at Harvard Medical School –
lived in this house during the mid
19th century. In 1849, in one of the
most sensationalized murder cases
in US history, Parkman was killed by
a faculty member, Dr. John Webster,
over a financial dispute. Both the
crime and its aftermath were grisly –
the ensuing trial saw the inclusion
of dental records as evidence for the
first time, as Parkman had been
partially cremated. The house is
now a city-owned meeting center

7 Boston Common

The oldest city park in the
country, the Common is a popular
gathering place for outdoor concerts,
public protests, picnics in summer
and, in the winter, ice-skating on
Frog Pond *(see pp18–19)*.

8 Beacon Street

MAP N3 ■ Boston Athenaeum:
10½ Beacon St ■ 617 227 7612 ■ Open
to the public noon–8pm Tue, 10am–
4pm Wed–Sat ■ Tours Tue, Thu & Sat,
by reservation ■ Adm

Beacon Street, in the blocks between
Somerset and Brimmer streets,
features the National Historic

BLACK HERITAGE TRAIL

By and large, America's history books are
dominated by white patriots such as Paul
Revere and John Adams. As a refreshing
counterpoint, the Black Heritage Trail
posits that black Bostonians, despite
their marginalized histories, have played
an indispensable role in the city's development. The trail illustrates this point at
every turn, taking visitors past the homes
and businesses of some of Boston's most
influential black Americans. Tours leave
from the Shaw Memorial at 10am and
1pm from July to Labor Day and at 1pm
from Labor Day to mid-October. Call a
day ahead to book (617 742 5415). www.
nps.gov/boaf)

Landmark Boston Athenaeum, one of the oldest independent libraries in the country, housed in a sumptuous building containing a collection of over 600,000 titles. Also here are the Massachusetts State House (see p15), Parkman House, and the Third Harrison Gray Otis House, at 45 Beacon St, considered architect Charles Bulfinch's finest Federal-style house. The facade of the former Bull and Finch Pub at 84 Beacon St is famed as the exterior of the bar in the TV show *Cheers*.

Boston Athenaeum library

⑨ George Middleton House
MAP N3 ■ 5–7 Pinckney St
■ Closed to the public

The oldest remaining private residence on Beacon Hill built by African-Americans is a highlight of the Black Heritage Trail. George Middleton, a Revolutionary War veteran, commissioned the house's construction soon after the war. Legend has it that he commanded an all-black company dubbed the "Bucks of America."

⑩ Boston's Center for Jewish Culture
MAP N2 ■ 13–18 Phillips St ■ 617 523 2324 ■ Open 11am–5pm Wed–Fri ■ www.vilnashul.com

The Vilna Shul testifies to the area's former vibrancy as Boston's first predominantly Jewish quarter. The congregation was founded in 1903 by immigrants who came from Vilna, Lithuania. It is now a center of Jewish culture with programs and exhibits.

BEACON HILL BY DAY

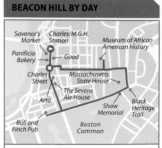

▶ MORNING

Take the "T" to the Charles Street/Massachusetts General Hospital stop and exit onto **Charles Street** (see p69). Enjoy a light breakfast at **Panificio Bakery** (144 Charles St) where the scones and muffins are out of this world. Then continue along Charles Street and turn right onto Beacon Street for a glimpse of the former **Bull and Finch Pub** – the bar that inspired the TV show *Cheers*. Continue up Beacon to the **Massachusetts State House** (see p81) for a free 45-minute weekday tour; times vary. Afterward, cross the road to the **Shaw Memorial** (see p18), from where National Park ranger-led **Black Heritage Trail** tours depart. The trail provides an excellent survey of the area's architectural styles as well as its black culture sites, and ends at the **Museum of African American History** (see p81).

AFTERNOON

Walk back down the hill to Charles Street for a fortifying late lunch. Weather permitting, stock up on fresh fruit, a crusty baguette, and a sampling of imported cheeses at the charming **Savenor's Market** (160 Charles St) and have a picnic on **Boston Common**. Or, for delicious Italian fare, try **Artù** (see p85). After lunch, peruse the sleek accessories, art, and design at **Good** (133 Charles St) and browse Charles Street's antique shops (see p84). Round the day off with a pint at **The Sevens Ale House** (see p85).

See map on p80 ←

Antiques and Gift Shops

Display at Devonia Antiques

1 Devonia Antiques
MAP M3 ■ 15 Charles St
■ Closed Tue

Head here for fine antique English porcelain and American and European stemware. Thousands of museum-quality and collector items are on display, including hand-painted cabinet plates, and individual pieces, as well as complete dinner services.

2 Eugene Galleries
MAP M3 ■ 76 Charles St
■ Closed Sun, Mon

This shop has an excellent and fascinating selection of antique books, maps, and prints, including many depicting the development and history of Boston.

3 Beacon Hill Chocolates
MAP M3
■ 91 Charles St

Handmade boxes of artisan chocolates, decorated with vintage Boston scenes, make ideal gifts. Don't miss the signature swirl of Caramel Sushi.

Beacon Hill Chocolates

4 20th Century Limited
MAP M3 ■ 73 Charles St

This shop specializes in vintage costume jewelry, but there's also handsome 1950s barware, vintage accessories, and other collectibles.

5 Boston Art & Antiques Company
MAP M3 ■ 119 Charles St

Twelve dealers operate in this lower-level space filled with treasures including Asian antiques, militaria, Impressionist landscape paintings, and much more.

6 Blackstone's of Beacon Hill
MAP M3 ■ 46 Charles St

This is the place to go for unique Boston-themed gifts such as *Make Way for Ducklings* pillows and ornaments, as well as high-quality Fenway Park mugs.

7 Elegant Findings
MAP M3 ■ 89 Charles St
■ Closed Tue, Wed & Sun

This intimate shop specializes in museum-quality, hand-painted 19th-century porcelain from all over Europe. You'll also find marble statuary, exquisite linens, and fine period furniture.

8 Upstairs Downstairs
MAP M3 ■ 93 Charles St

This cozy shop places a refreshing emphasis on affordability and function. Everything from mahogany four-poster beds to *belle époque* opera glasses is on display.

9 Marika's Antiques
MAP M3 ■ 130 Charles St ■ Closed Sun & Mon

Packed to its dusty rafters with oil paintings, tarnished silverware, and mismatched china – nothing quite beats that thrill of discovery you'll find here.

10 Good
MAP M3 ■ 98 Charles St

While many Beacon Hill shops evoke the city's elite Brahmin past, Good specializes in unique contemporary designs, which include handmade jewelry, apparel, and accessories.

Restaurants and Bars

PRICE CATEGORIES

For a three course meal for one with half a bottle of wine (or equivalent meal), taxes, and extra charges.

$ under $40 $$ $40–$60 $$$ over $60

1 Mooo
MAP P3 ▪ 15 Beacon St
▪ 617 670 2515 ▪ $$$

Mooo specializes in extraordinary beef and classic accompaniments at expense-account prices. The wine list includes many stellar names.

2 City Winery
MAP G3 ▪ 80 Beverly St
▪ 617 933 8047 ▪ $$

This stylish wine bar (see p61) boasts an on-site winery, a shop and a concert space, which hosts live music performances every night.

3 Beacon Hill Pub
MAP M2 ▪ 149 Charles St
▪ 617 523 1895

This popular cash only, no-frills bar represents a holdout of pre-gentrification on Beacon Hill. Beer flows freely and patrons adore the foosball table and arcade games.

4 Alibi
MAP F3 ▪ Liberty Hotel, 215 Charles St ▪ 857 241 1144 ▪ $$$

Located within the Liberty Hotel, the trendy Alibi is a good spot for cocktails (see p61). The hotel also houses Scampo, a chic restaurant with a modern Italian-accented menu.

5 The Sevens Ale House
MAP M3 ▪ 77 Charles St

The epitome of a local Boston bar: dark wood, slightly surly staff, amiable patrons, a dartboard, and a rudimentary pub menu.

6 21st Amendment
MAP G3 ▪ 150 Bowdoin St

This neighborhood pub near the State House is a classy spot for legislators to indulge in a tipple or two.

7 Lala Rokh
MAP N3 ▪ 97 Mount Vernon St
▪ 617 720 5511 ▪ Closed L Sat & Sun
▪ $$

Authentic Persian cuisine is served in this casual spot. Citrus-based glazes and relishes give meats amazing piquant flavor.

8 Artù
MAP M3 ▪ 89 Charles St
▪ 617 227 9023 ▪ Closed L Sun–Tue
▪ $$$

Tuscan specialties such as *porchetta*, lamb cutlets, spicy seafood, and roasted vegetables come sizzling off the grill straight to your table.

Dining area at Beacon Hill Bistro

9 Beacon Hill Bistro
MAP M3 ▪ 25 Charles St ▪ 617 723 1133 ▪ Open for brunch Sat & Sun, closed L Sat & Sun ▪ $$$

This kitchen in the Beacon Hill Hotel puts an American stamp on French bistro cuisine to great effect.

10 75 Chestnut
MAP M3 ▪ 75 Chestnut St
▪ 617 227 2175 ▪ Closed L except Sat & Sun brunch ▪ $$

This converted townhouse offers one of Beacon Hill's most popular drinking and dining hangouts for brunch and dinner. The menu offers affordable American bistro dishes.

See map on p80 ←

🔟 Back Bay

Interior of Boston Public Library

The easily navigated grid of streets in Back Bay bears little resemblance to the labyrinthine lanes around Downtown and the North End. In the mid-1800s, Back Bay was filled in to accommodate Boston's mushrooming population and, by the late 1800s, the area had become a vibrant, upscale neighborhood. Home to many of Boston's wealthiest families, the area was characterized by lavish houses, grand churches, and bustling commercial zones. Many of the original buildings stand intact, providing an exquisite 19th-century backdrop for today's pulsing nightlife, world-class shopping, and sumptuous dining.

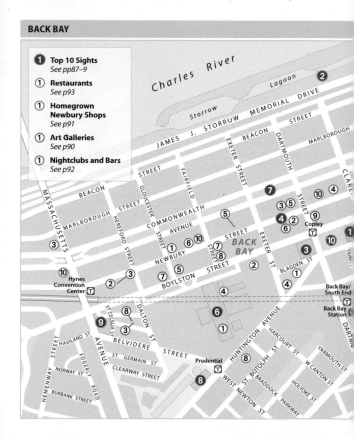

BACK BAY

- **1** Top 10 Sights
  See pp87–9
- **1** Restaurants
  See p93
- **1** Homegrown
  Newbury Shops
  See p91
- **1** Art Galleries
  See p90
- **1** Nightclubs and Bars
  See p92

1 Trinity Church

When I. M. Pei's 60-story John Hancock Tower was completed in 1976, Bostonians feared that Trinity Church would be overshadowed by its gleaming upstart neighbor. Yet H. H. Richardson's masterpiece, dedicated in 1877, remains just as vital to Copley Square, and as beautiful, as it was on its opening day (see pp32–3).

2 The Esplanade
MAP M3

The perfect setting for a leisurely bike ride, invigorating jog, or a lazy afternoon of soaking up the sun, the Esplanade is one of the city's most popular green spaces. This ribbon of green hugging the Charles' riverbanks was inspired by Venetian canals.

View from the Esplanade

Fourth of July (see p73) at the Esplanade's Hatch Shell brings the world-famous Boston Pops Orchestra along with thousands of revelers to enjoy the incomparable mix of music, good cheer, and awe-inspiring fireworks. Use caution if on the esplanade at night.

3 Boston Public Library
MAP I 5 ■ 700 Boylston St ■ 617 536 5400 ■ Open 9am–9pm Mon–Thu, 9am–5pm Fri & Sat, 1–5pm Sun (Jun–Sep: closed Sun) ■ Tours 2:30pm Mon, 6pm Tue & Thu, 11am Wed, Fri & Sat, 2pm Sun ■ www.bpl.org

Although this McKim, Mead, & White-designed building opened in 1895, the Boston Public Library was founded in 1848 as the country's first publicly funded library. Lavish stone and marble interiors and gleaming oak woodwork make it a "palace of the people." A series of murals illustrate the value placed on public education when the library was constructed. Its courtyard restaurant serves afternoon tea. Guided tours offer insight into the building's architecture and history.

4 Newbury Street

Over the years, Back Bay's most famous street has proven to be amazingly adaptable, with fashion boutiques blending seamlessly into their mid-19th-century brownstone environs. This is the liveliest, most eclectic street in Boston: a babble of languages, skater punks alongside catwalk models, and delivery trucks and Ferraris jockeying for the same parking space (see pp24–5).

0 meters 250
0 yards 250

5 Gibson House Museum
MAP M4 ▪ 137 Beacon St
▪ 617 267 6338 ▪ Tours 1pm, 2pm, & 3pm Wed–Sun ▪ Adm ▪ www.thegibsonhouse.org

One of the first private residences to be built in Back Bay (c.1859), Gibson House remains beautifully intact. The house has been preserved as a monument to the era, thanks largely to the efforts of its final resident (the grandson of the well-to-do woman who built the house). So frozen in time does this house appear that you might feel like you're intruding on someone's inner sanctum, and an earlier age. Highlights of the tour include some elegant porcelain dinnerware, 18th-century heirloom jewelry, and exquisite black walnut woodwork throughout the house.

6 Prudential Center
MAP K6 ▪ 800 Boylston St
▪ 617 236 3100 ▪ Stores open 10am–9pm Mon–Sat, 11am–7pm Sun

Although it's difficult to imagine, the Prudential Tower's 52 stories seem dwarfed by the huge swath of street-level shops and restaurants that constitute the Prudential Center. With its indoor shopping mall, eateries, supermarket, cluster of residential towers, and massive convention center, the Prudential Center is like a self-contained city within a city. For a jaw-dropping view of Boston, visit the Skywalk on the tower's 50th level (see p53), or the Top of the Hub Lounge (see p92), two floors above.

Statues on Commonwealth Avenue

7 Commonwealth Avenue
MAP J5–L4

With its leafy pedestrian mall and *belle époque*-inspired architecture, Commonwealth Avenue aptly deserves its comparison to *les rues parisiennes*. A morning jog on the mall is a popular pastime, as is the occasional picnic or afternoon snooze on a bench. Highlights include Boston's First Baptist Church (110 Commonwealth; closed to non-worshipers) and the pedestrian mall's stately statues, including the William Lloyd Garrison bronze, sculpted by Olin Levi Warner.

8 Christian Science Center
MAP K6 ▪ 175 Huntington Ave
▪ 617 450 7000 ▪ Library open 10am–4pm Tue–Sun ▪ Adm for Mapparium ▪ www.marybakereddylibrary.org

While believers head for the Romanesque-Byzantine basilica, the library (entered from Massachusetts Avenue) emphasizes inspirational facets of the life of the founder (see pp44–5) rather than church doctrine.

Christian Science Center and the Prudential Center

The Mapparium, a walk-through stained-glass globe with 1935 political boundaries, remains the most popular exhibit *(see p50)*. Admire the Neo-Classical lobby of the *Christian Science Monitor*. Outside, a 670-ft (204-m) reflecting pool, designed by I. M. Pei, is lined with begonias, marigolds, and columbines.

⑨ Berklee Performance Center

MAP J6 ▪ 136 Massachusetts Ave ▪ 617 747 2261 ▪ Check website for details of concerts and performances ▪ www.berklee.edu/BPC

The largest independent music school in the world, Berklee was founded in 1945. The college has produced a number of world-renowned jazz, rock, and pop stars, including Quincy Jones, Melissa Etheridge, Kevin Eubanks, Jan Hammer, and Branford Marsalis. The state-of-the-art performance center hosts concerts by students, faculty, and visiting artists.

⑩ Copley Square

MAP L5

Named after John Singleton Copley, the renowned 18th-century Boston painter, Copley Square is surrounded by some of the city's most striking architectural gems, notably Trinity Church and the Boston Public Library. A hub of activities, the bustling square hosts weekly farmers' markets, concerts, and folk dance shows in summer. The BosTix booth sells discounted tickets for theater, music, and dance performances.

EXPLORING BACK BAY

Public Garden
Fresh
Ben & Jerry's
Trident Booksellers & Café
Trinity Church
Bistro du Midi
Boston Public Library
Fairmont Copley Plaza
Prudential Center, Top of the Hub Lounge

▶ AFTERNOON

Enjoy a *croque monsieur* or *moules frites* at the **Bistro du Midi** *(272 Boylston St)* while gazing out onto the **Public Garden** *(see pp18–19)*. Stroll one block over to Newbury Street *(see pp24–5)* and take in the impressive contemporary art galleries concentrated between Arlington and Dartmouth streets. Then cross back over to Boylston at Dartmouth and sit for a while inside **Trinity Church** *(see pp32–3)* where La Farge's stained-glass windows top an inexhaustible list of highlights. And while you're in an aesthetics-appreciating mood, traverse St. James Place to the **Fairmont Copley Plaza** hotel *(see p148)* and lounge for a few minutes in the ornate, Versailles-esque lobby. Next, cross Dartmouth to the **Boston Public Library** *(see p87)* and admire John Singer Sargent's gorgeous murals.

Now it's time to warm up your credit card, so head back to Newbury Street for a dizzying shopping spree. Turn left onto Newbury for Boston-only boutiques such as **Fresh** *(see p91)* and **Trident Booksellers & Café** *(see p91)*. Pause for a reinvigorating fruit smoothie or towering sundae at **Ben & Jerry's** (174 Newbury St). At Massachusetts Avenue, turn left, then left again onto Boylston and continue to the **Prudential Center** for name-brand shopping – you'll find Saks Fifth Avenue, Lord & Taylor, and the like. Cap it all off with a bracing-cold cocktail and smooth jazz at the 52nd-floor **Top of the Hub Lounge** *(see p92)*, where you can soak in Boston's skyline – and, with any luck, a dazzling sunset.

See map on pp86–7

Art Galleries

1 Robert Klein
MAP M5 ▪ 38 Newbury St
▪ 617 267 7997 ▪ Closed Sun & Mon

Everybody who's anybody in photography vies for space at Robert Klein. Past coups include shows by Annie Leibovitz and Herb Ritts.

2 Copley Society of Art
MAP L5 ▪ 158 Newbury St
▪ 617 536 5049 ▪ Closed Mon

With a commitment to exhibiting works by promising New England artists, this non-profit organization has been providing young artists with that crucial first break since 1879.

3 Childs Gallery
MAP TK ▪ 169 Newbury St ▪ 617 266 1108 ▪ Closed Mon

The Childs Gallery was founded in 1937 and displays an eclectic range of paintings, drawings and sculpture. Don't miss the print department in the basement.

4 Krakow Witkin Gallery
MAP M5 ▪ 10 Newbury St
▪ 617 262 4490 ▪ Closed Sun & Mon; Aug

Since opening in 1964, this gallery has championed contemporary artists who create conceptually driven and minimalist work.

Work by Jackie Ferrara, Krakow Witkin Gallery

5 DTR Modern Galleries
MAP L5 ▪ 167 Newbury St
▪ 617 424 9700

DTR champions modern and contemporary art with an inventory that ranges from Salvador Dalí to Andy Warhol and Keith Haring.

6 Guild of Boston Artists
MAP L5 ▪ 162 Newbury St
▪ 617 536 7660 ▪ Closed Sun & Mon

The skylit gallery space exhibits representational painting and sculpture by New England artists. More than 40 artists founded the guild in 1914.

7 Gallery NAGA
MAP M5 ▪ 67 Newbury St ▪ 617 267 9060 ▪ Closed Sun & Mon; Jul & Aug

Representing some of New England's best regarded artists, NAGA is possibly Newbury's top contemporary art gallery.

Sculpture outside Vose Galleries

8 Pucker Gallery
MAP K5 ▪ 240 Newbury St, 3rd floor
▪ 617 267 9473

You never know what you might discover in this gallery that embraces work in a variety of media created by US and international artists.

9 Vose Galleries
MAP K5 ▪ 238 Newbury St
▪ 617 536 6176 ▪ Closed Sun & Mon

The oldest art gallery in the US, Vose specializes in American realist painting and works on paper from the 18th–20th centuries.

10 Arden Gallery
MAP L5 ▪ 129 Newbury St
▪ 617 247 0610 ▪ Closed Sun

This gallery focuses on original paintings and sculpture, including those cast in bronze and other metals. It also showcases up-and-coming abstract and realist artists.

Homegrown Newbury Shops

 Johnny Cupcakes
MAP K6 ■ 279 Newbury St

This boutique specializes in limited-edition crossbones-and-cupcake T-shirts. The joke continues with bakery case displays, aprons on the staff, and the smell of cake batter in the air.

 Trident Booksellers & Café
MAP K6 ■ 338 Newbury St

Trident is popular for its delicious, healthy sandwiches, strong coffee concoctions, and what is arguably the best book and magazine selection in the city.

Display at Newbury Comics

 Newbury Comics
MAP J6 ■ 332 Newbury St

Generally undercutting the chain stores on CDs, Newbury Comics delivers value along with a stellar selection of rare import CDs and a growing range of exclusive, rare and vintage vinyl, as well as concert videos, and the latest comics.

4 Fresh
MAP L5 ■ 121 Newbury St

Fresh sells chic grooming products for men and women, many of them based on such natural products as sugar (for face and body skin polish), clay (masks and lotions), and soy (facial cleaning gel).

 **Hempest**
MAP K5 ■ 301 Newbury St

A true believer in the superiority of hemp as something to wear rather than inhale, Hempest showcases chic and casual styles fashioned from this environmentally friendly fiber.

6 Boston Olive Oil Company
MAP K5 ■ 253 Newbury St

This family-owned shop offers more than 60 premium varieties of Extra Virgin olive oil and balsamic vinegars.

 Shreve, Crump & Low
MAP M5 ■ 39 Newbury St

First opened in 1796 near Paul Revere's silversmith shop, this fine jeweler is a Boston institution, renowned for its engagement rings. But the "gurgling cod" jugs make a whimsical and less pricey gift.

8 Concepts
MAP J6 ■ 73 Newbury St

This small shop stocks an impressive collection of sneakers, street wear and designer clothing, ranging from Adidas and Vans to Jimmy Choo and Giuseppe Zanotti.

9 Simon Pearce
MAP F4 ■ 103 Newbury St

Fine blown glass and handmade pottery from this eponymous Irish designer and artist creates tableware with an upscale touch. Pearce signatures include classic goblets and other stemware.

10 Deluca's Back Bay Market
MAP K5 ■ 239 Newbury St

This old world-style corner market stocks fabulous produce, chilled beer, ready-made sandwiches, and imported delights of all kinds.

See map on pp86–7

Nightclubs and Bars

 Top of the Hub Lounge
MAP K6 ■ Prudential Tower,
800 Boylston St

Talk about a view: 52 stories above Back Bay, this bar dazzles with sweeping views, live jazz, deliciously sophisticated lounge food menu, and a wicked gin martini.

 Oak Long Bar & Kitchen
MAP L6 ■ 138 St James Ave

This award-winning bar (see p60) in the historic Copley Plaza (see p148) exudes old-school class and charm.

3 Kings
MAP J6 ■ 10 Scotia St

The 1950s were never so cool as they seem at this retro-styled lounge, pool hall, and bowling alley buried downstairs next to the Hynes Convention Center.

4 Storyville
MAP F5 ■ 94 Exeter St ■ Closed Sun–Tue, Thu

Speakeasy meets nightclub at this lounge which serves hip bar food such as short rib casserole, and snazzy cocktails.

5 Whiskey's
MAP K6 ■ 885 Boylston St

This lively bar is full of hard-drinking collegiate types, who arrive around 6pm and stay until last call. It also serves reasonably priced bar bites and great buffalo wings and burgers.

 Bar at the Taj
MAP F4 ■ 15 Arlington St
■ Closes 11:30pm, 12:30am Fri & Sat

Boston's elite have been socializing at this elegant room facing the Public Garden since the 1920s.

 The Pour House
MAP K6 ■ 907 Boylston St

Cheap, hearty pub grub and occasional drink specials lure college kids to this two-story bar and grill. It's loud, it's crowded, and you're bound to make a friend or two.

 Bukowski Tavern
MAP K6 ■ 50 Dalton St

A beer drinker's paradise, Bukowski counts 100 varieties of the beverage. Its primary patrons are a professional crowd during the day and young hipsters at night.

9 Lolita Cocina & Tequila Bar
MAP L5 ■ 271 Dartmouth St

There's always a festive mood at this trendy, Gothic-styled bar. Choose from the long list of specialty tequilas, accompanied by Mexican food.

 Bristol Bar
MAP N4 ■ 200 Boylston St
■ Closes 1am

Sharing room with the excellent Bristol Lounge, this sophisticated bar in the Four Seasons hotel charms visitors with its signature martinis.

Whiskey's, located in the heart of Back Bay

Restaurants

PRICE CATEGORIES
For a three-course meal for one with half
a bottle of wine (or equivalent meal),
taxes, and extra charges.

$ under $40 $$ $40–$60 $$$ over $60

1 Sorellina
MAP F5 ▪ 1 Huntington Ave
▪ 617 412 4600 ▪ $$$

Regional Italian food with a contem-
porary spin is accompanied by a
range of great wines and served up
in a sophisticated dining room.

2 L'Espalier
MAP K6 ▪ 774 Boylston St
▪ 617 262 3023 ▪ $$$

New England ingredients combine
with high-style modern French
technique to create memorable,
luxury dining.

3 Deuxave
MAP E5 ▪ 371 Commonwealth
Ave ▪ 617 517 5915 ▪ Closed L ▪ $$$

Elegant contemporary dining ranges
from local lobster and scallops to
caramelized onion ravioli. In sum-
mer, outside seating is available.

4 Eataly
MAP K6 ▪ 800 Boylston St
▪ 617 807 7300 ▪ $–$$$

This vast emporium of all foods
Italian includes more than a dozen
different dining venues amid the
groceries and kitchen gadgets.

5 Post 390
MAP M5 ▪ 406 Stuart St ▪ 617
399 0015 ▪ Closed L Sat & Sun ▪ $$$

This urban tavern near the South
End border is a comfortable meeting
spot, with three fireplaces, two bars,
and an open kitchen on two levels.

6 Mistral
MAP M6 ▪ 223 Columbus Ave
▪ 617 867 9300 ▪ $$$

Delectable French-Mediterranean
dishes and an excellent wine list
make Mistral an ideal dining venue.

Entrance to Grill 23 & Bar

7 Grill 23 & Bar
MAP M5 ▪ 161 Berkeley St
▪ 617 542 2255 ▪ Closed L ▪ $$$

Grill 23 harkens back to the days
of exclusive, Prohibition-era supper
clubs. Prime aged beef with an
inventive spin is served in a
sumptuous classic interior.

8 Brasserie Jo
MAP K6 ▪ 120 Huntington
Ave ▪ 617 425 3240 ▪ $$$

Bustling Brasserie Jo captures
the *savoir faire* of 1940s Paris.
Relish hearty French classics
like steak roquefort.

9 Erbaluce
MAP G5 ▪ 69 Church St
▪ 617 426 6969 ▪ $$$

Chef Charles Draghi brings French
technical finesse to north Italian
cuisine with a menu that changes
nightly. Excellent, all-Italian wine list.

10 Uni
MAP J5 ▪ 370A Commonwealth
Ave ▪ 617 536 7200 ▪ Closed L & Mon
▪ $$$

Contemporary Japanese cuisine
rules at this fine-dining izakaya
restaurant. Late-night weekend
ramen draws a crowd.

See map on pp86–7

TOP 10 North End and the Waterfront

The North End is Boston's Italian village, where one feast day blends into the next all summer as the great-grandchildren of the original immigrants celebrate the music, food, and dolce vita of the old

Old North Church road marker

country. Yet the North End predates its Italian inhabitants and the neighborhood is in fact the oldest in Boston. The area along the waterfront bristles with condo developments on former shipping piers, which lead south to the bustle of Long, Central, and Rowes wharves. Boston was born by the sea and it is now reclaiming its waterfront as a vital center for business and pleasure.

NORTH END AND THE WATERFRONT

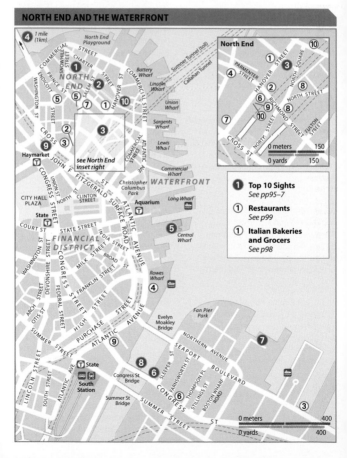

1. **Top 10 Sights**
   See pp95–7

1. **Restaurants**
   See p99

1. **Italian Bakeries and Grocers**
   See p98

1 Copp's Hill Burying Ground

MAP Q1 ■ Hull St ■ 617 635 4505
■ Open 9am–5pm daily

Trace the history of Boston on the thousands of tombstones found here *(see p13)*, from the mean-spirited Mather family, who were theocrats who ruled the early city of the late 17th and 18th century, to the valiant patriots slain in the fight for freedom during the American Revolution. In the Battle of Bunker Hill *(see p14)*, the British, who occupied the city in 1775, manned a battery from this site and fired on neighboring Charlestown. There are sweeping views of the harbor.

2 Old North Church

MAP Q1 ■ 193 Salem St ■ 617 858 8231 ■ Open Apr–Nov: 9am–6pm daily (shorter hours off-season) ■ Adm ■ www.oldnorth.com

An active Episcopal congregation still worships at Boston's oldest church, officially known as Christ Church (1723). It was here, in 1775, that sexton Robert Newman hung two lanterns in the belfry to warn horseback messenger Paul Revere of British troop movements, an event commemorated by a bronze plaque in the street outside *(see p14)*.

Exterior of Paul Revere House

3 Paul Revere House

MAP Q1 ■ 19 North Sq
■ 617 523 2338 ■ Open mid-Apr–Oct: 9:30am–5:15pm daily; Nov–mid Apr: 9:30am–4:15pm daily (closed Mon Jan–Mar) ■ Adm ■ www.paulrevere house.org

Home to Paul Revere for 30 years, this 17th-century clapboard house is the only surviving home of any of Boston's revolutionary heroes. It provides an intriguing glimpse into the domestic life of Revere's family with displays of their furniture and possessions, including silverwork made by Revere, who was highly regarded as a metalsmith. Well-trained staff tell the tale of Revere's legendary midnight ride *(see p14)*.

4 Charlestown Navy Yard

MAP H2

One of the original six naval yards created to support the fledgling US Navy, the Charlestown Navy Yard *(see pp36–7)* was a center of technical innovation. The heart of the yard opened as a historic site in 1974. Its two most popular exhibits include the famous USS *Constitution* frigate, and the World War II era destroyer USS *Cassin Young*.

5 New England Aquarium

Now the centerpiece of the downtown waterfront development, the aquarium's construction in the 1960s paved the way for the revital-ization of Boston Harbor as a whole. Harbor seals cavort in a tank in front of the sleek structure *(see pp38–9)*.

Interior of Old North Church

Exterior of the Children's Museum

6 Children's Museum

MAP R5 ■ 308 Congress St
■ 617 426 6500 ■ Open 10am–5pm
daily, to 9pm Fri ■ Adm ■ www.
bostonchildrensmuseum.org

This interactive museum is the
perfect place to take the family
for hands-on fun (see p52).

7 Institute of Contemporary Art

25 Harbor Shore Dr ■ 617 478 3100
■ Open 10am–5pm Tue, Wed, Sat &
Sun, 10am–9pm Thu & Fri ■ Adm
■ www.icaboston.org

The ICA was founded in 1936 and
reopened in its modern landmark
structure on Fan Pier in 2006. The
striking glass, wood, and steel
building, designed by Diller Scofidio +
Renfro, is cantilevered over the
HarborWalk and provides dramatic
views. The ICA promotes cutting-
edge art and focuses on 21st-century
work. There is also a program of
performing arts and other events,
with waterfront concerts in summer.

**Harborside setting of the Boston Tea
Party Ships and Museum**

FORAGING FOR FORMAGGIO

Italian food, wine, and culture expert
Michele Topor has lived in the North
End for four decades. Her tour of the
local markets of Boston's "Little Italy"
on Wednesday and Saturday (10am
and 2pm), and Friday (10am and 3pm)
includes tastings and insights on local
restaurants. To reserve a place, contact
Boston Food Tours: 800 656 0713,
www.bostonfoodtours.com.

8 Boston Tea Party Ships and Museum

MAP R5 ■ Congress St Bridge ■ 617
338 1773 ■ Open 10am–5pm daily
(closes 4pm in winter) ■ Adm
■ www.bostonteapartyship.com

The historic occasion known as the
Boston Tea Party, when patriots
dressed as Native Americans and
threw a consignment of English tea
overboard to protest against the
Stamp Tax of 1773, proved to be a
catalyst of the American Revolution
(see p14). The Boston Tea Party ships
are replicas of the vessels that were
relieved of their cargo that fateful
December night. Costumed
storytellers recount events in rousing
detail, and visitors can board one of
the vessels and even participate in a
re-enactment of the destruction. In
the museum is one of two tea crates
known to have survived from the
incident, while
Abigail's Tea
Room serves
up a nice
"cuppa."

⑨ Rose Kennedy Greenway

MAP P1 ■ www.rosekennedy
greenway.org

The Greenway is a ribbon of organic, contemporary parkland through the heart of Boston, where visitors and locals laze on the lawns, cool off in the fountains, buy lunch at one of the affordable food trucks, and enjoy free Wi-Fi. There's a charming carousel featuring local hand-carved wildlife, with cod, lobster, rabbit, and more. Artworks include the Harbor Fog water sculpture, near Rowes Wharf, which evokes the sea with fog, light, and sound, as well as installations that change every year. Colorful garden plants punctuate the park's walkways.

Rose Kennedy Greenway

⑩ St. Stephen's Church

MAP R1 ■ 401 Hanover St ■ 617 523 1230 ■ Open 8:30am–4:30pm Mon–Sat, 11am Sun for worship

Renowned architect Charles Bulfinch completely redesigned St. Stephen's original 1714 structure in 1802–4, and the church is the only surviving example of his religious architecture. Its bell was cast by Paul Revere. The complex Neo-Classical exterior contrasts with the open, airy, and relatively unadorned interior. In 1862, the Roman Catholic archdiocese took over the church to accommodate the area's growing number of Irish immigrants. Rose Fitzgerald, daughter of Boston mayor and St. Stephen's parishioner John "Honey Fitz" Fitzgerald, and mother of President John F. Kennedy (see p45), is linked to the church. She was baptized here in 1890, and her funeral took place here in 1995.

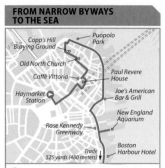

**FROM NARROW BYWAYS
TO THE SEA**

Copp's Hill Burying Ground · Puopolo Park · Old North Church · Caffè Vittoria · Haymarket Station · Paul Revere House · Joe's American Bar & Grill · New England Aquarium · Rose Kennedy Greenway · Trade · Boston Harbour Hotel

525 yards (480 meters)

▶ MORNING

From the Haymarket "T", follow Hanover Street to Richmond Street and continue to North Square. Stop at **Paul Revere House** (see p95) for a glimpse into the domestic life of the revolutionary hero. Return to Hanover for an espresso and some prime people-watching at lively **Caffè Vittoria** (see p66). Continue up Hanover and turn left through Paul Revere Mall to **Old North Church** (see p95). The bust of George Washington inside is reputedly the world's most accurate rendering of his face – compare the resemblance to a dollar bill. Then stroll up Hull Street past Copp's Hill Burying Ground (see p95) for a great view of USS Constitution (see p36) and continue to the waterfront. Grab a bench in **Puopolo Park** (see p47) to watch a match of bocce. Walk south along Commercial Street and stop for an alfresco waterside lunch at **Joe's American Bar & Grill** (100 Atlantic Ave).

AFTERNOON

Resume your waterfront stroll, admiring the views of the harbor as you walk. Then stop off to enjoy the roses in the **Rose Kennedy Greenway**, before whiling away an hour or so in the **New England Aquarium** (see pp38–9) where highlights include the swirling Giant Ocean Tank. Relax with a sundowner on the patio of the **Boston Harbor Hotel** (see p146) before you head to **Trade** (see p99) for dinner.

See map on p94 ←

Italian Bakeries and Grocers

1 Mike's Pastry

MAP Q1 ■ 300 Hanover St

Large glass cases display a huge selection of cookies and *cannoli* (crunchy pastry filled with a sweet ricotta cream). Purchase a box to go, or grab a table and order a drink and a delectable pastry.

2 Salumeria Italiana

MAP Q2

■ 151 Richmond St

This neighborhood fixture is a great source of esoteric Italian canned goods and rich olive oils, as well as spicy sausages and cheeses from many Italian regions.

Modern Pastry shop sign

3 Maria's Pastry Shop

MAP Q2 ■ 46 Cross St

Run for three generations by the Merola family, Maria's is famed for its Neapolitan flaky and sweet *sfogliatelle* (filled pastry) as well as seasonal sweets, such as chocolate-allspice cookies at Christmas and marzipan lambs at Easter.

4 Polcari's Coffee Co.
MAP Q1 ■ 105 Salem St

■ Closed Sun

The premier bulk grocer in the North End, this charming store has sold fine Italian roasted coffee since 1932. It's still the best place to find spices, flours, grains, and legumes.

Coffee beans at Polcari's Coffee Co.

5 Bova's Bakery

MAP Q1 ■ 134 Salem St

Fresh bread emerges from the ovens at all hours. When the coffee shops and bars close, head to Bova's for hot sandwiches and cookies.

6 Modern Pastry
MAP Q2 ■ 257 Hanover St

The house specialties here include a rich ricotta pie, delicious florentines, and nougat, which are all made on the premises, as well as chocolate truffles from Italy. Modern makes a thinner *cannoli* shell than Mike's.

7 Monica's Mercato

MAP Q1 ■ 130 Salem St

Linked to a nearby restaurant, this *salumeria* has all the usual cheeses and sausages, but its specialties are prepared foods such as cold salads for picnics and pasta dishes for reheating.

8 V. Cirace Wine & Spirits
MAP Q2 ■ 173 North St

■ Closed Sun

The North End's most upscale seller of Italian wines and liqueurs stocks both fine wines to lay down and cheerfully youthful ones to enjoy right away.

9 Bricco Panetteria

MAP Q2 ■ 241 Hanover St

This subterranean bakery turns out amazing Italian and French breads day and night. Follow the delicious smells to find it tucked down an alley.

10 Bricco Salumeria & Pasta Shop
MAP Q2 ■ 11 Board Alley

With many varieties of fresh pasta made daily, plus sauces, pesto, grating cheeses, and a handful of hard-to-find Italian groceries, this North End takeout is ideal for stocking up a picnic basket.

Restaurants

PRICE CATEGORIES
For a three-course meal for one with half a bottle of wine (or equivalent meal), taxes, and extra charges.

$ under $40 $$ $40–$60 $$$ over $60

Maurizio's
MAP Q1 ■ 364 Hanover St ■ 617 367 1123 ■ $$

At this cozy, buzzy spot, chef Maurizio Lodo draws on his Sardinian heritage to create inventive and comforting dishes that often feature fish. Wines are carefully selected to complement the food.

Seafood at Neptune Oyster

Neptune Oyster
MAP Q1 ■ 63 Salem St ■ 617 742 3474 ■ $$

The delicate raw bar oysters are almost upstaged by large and bold roasted fish and pasta dishes in this tiny, stylish spot. Tables turn quickly.

3 Legal Harborside
MAP H3 ■ Liberty Wharf and other locations ■ 617 477 2900 ■ $$$

The flagship of the Legal Sea Foods chain offers three floors of seafood heaven. It's popular, so book ahead.

4 Meritage
MAP H4 ■ 70 Rowes Wharf ■ 617 439 3995 ■ $$$

The innovative menu at this sleek, waterfront restaurant (see p63) is driven by an excellent and varied selection of wines.

5 Pizzeria Regina
MAP Q1 ■ 11½ Thatcher St ■ $

Founded in 1926, the original, family-run Regina offers brick-oven, thin-crust, old-fashioned pizza, which is far better than the pale imitations served at its other branches.

6 Menton
MAP H5 ■ 354 Congress St ■ 617 737 0099 ■ Closed L ■ $$$

Barbara Lynch's luxurious restaurant (see p63) serves seasonally inspired dishes such as East Coast halibut, dry-aged ribeye and crab bisque. Try the excellent four-course prix fixe menu or the chef's tasting menu.

7 Taranta
MAP Q2 ■ 210 Hanover St ■ 617 720 0052 ■ Closed L Sun ■ $$$

A creative and unusual blend of Sardinian and Peruvian cuisine spells intense flavors in dishes such as pork with vinegar peppers and broccoli.

8 Mamma Maria
MAP H3 ■ 3 North Sq ■ 617 523 0077 ■ Closed L ■ $$$

Set in a romantic 19th-century row house, Mamma Maria (see p62) specializes in northern Italian cuisine, with a few Sicilian and Neapolitan dishes. The extensive wine list is excellent.

9 Trade
MAP H4 ■ 540 Atlantic Ave ■ 617 451 1234 ■ $$$

This airy upscale restaurant (see p62) evokes Boston's global shipping days with its superb, eclectic world cuisine and creative cocktails.

10 Prezza
MAP R1 ■ 24 Fleet St ■ 617 227 1577 ■ Closed L, Sun ■ $$$

With one of the longest wine lists in town, Prezza is bound to offer just the right glass to accompany its hearty Tuscan fare as well as its sinfully rich desserts.

See map on p94 ←

🔟 Downtown and the Financial District

Old Granary Burying Ground

The heart of Boston lies between Boston Common and the harbor. Boston has great respect for its past and there are reminders of history embedded in the center of this metropolis. The 18th-century grace of the Old State House still shines within a canyon of skyscrapers. The heroes of Boston's early years – city founder John Winthrop, patriot Paul Revere, and revolutionary Samuel Adams – are buried just steps from sidewalks abuzz with shoppers. Rolled in to this area is the Financial District as well as Boston's oldest commercial district, Faneuil Hall and Quincy Market.

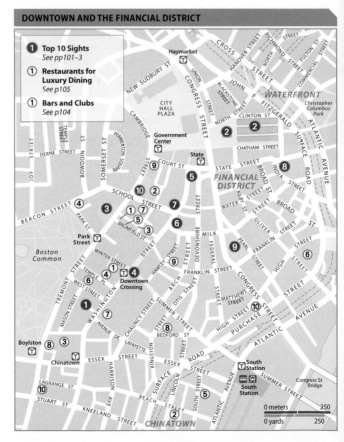

DOWNTOWN AND THE FINANCIAL DISTRICT

1 **Top 10 Sights**
  See pp101–3

1 **Restaurants for Luxury Dining**
  See p105

1 **Bars and Clubs**
  See p104

Brattle Book Shop, Ladder District

1 Ladder District
MAP P4

The network of short streets linking Washington and Tremont streets has assumed a modern identity as the Ladder District. Once derelict and abandoned after dark, the area is now filled with bars and restaurants. Anchoring the district are the ultra-chic Millennium Tower that overlooks Boston Common (see pp18–19), the Ritz-Carlton, and the top-of-the-line AMC Loews cineplex (175 Tremont St). A few stalwarts, such as landmark bookseller Brattle Book Shop, are holding out against the big boys.

2 Faneuil Hall and Quincy Market
MAP Q2 ■ 1 Faneuil Hall Square ■ Open Faneuil Hall: 9am–5pm daily; Quincy Market: 10am–9pm Mon–Sat, 11am–7pm Sun ■ www.faneuilhallmarketplace.com

Many a fiery speech urging revolution echoed in Faneuil Hall in the late 18th century; in the 1820s it was the city's food distribution that was revolutionized in adjacent Quincy Market. Today the buildings and surrounding plazas form a shopping and dining destination – the model for dozens of markets worldwide.

3 Old Granary Burying Ground
MAP P3 ■ Tremont St at Park St ■ 617 635 4505 ■ Open 9am–5pm daily

Dating from 1660, the Granary contains the graves of many of Boston's most illustrious figures, including John Hancock, Samuel Adams, and Paul Revere (see p44), who joined his revolutionary comrades here in 1818. Other notables include Declaration of Independence signatory Robert Treat Paine, the parents of Benjamin Franklin, and Crispus Attucks – an escaped slave who was the first casualty of the Boston Massacre (see p14).

4 Downtown Crossing
MAP P4 ■ Junction of Summer, Winter, and Washington Sts

This pedestrian-friendly shopping area is dominated by Macy's department store. Pushcart vendors offer more quirky goods, and food carts provide quick lunches for Downtown office workers.

5 Old State House
MAP Q3 ■ Washington & State Sts ■ 617 720 1713 ■ Open 9am–5pm daily (late May–early Sep: until 6pm) ■ Adm ■ www.bostonhistory.org

Built in 1713 as the seat of colonial government, the Old State House was sited to look down State Street to the shipping hub of Long Wharf. In 1770, the Boston Massacre (see p14) occurred outside its doors, and on July 18, 1776, the Declaration of Independence was first read to Bostonians from its balcony. Today, it's home to the Bostonian Society and Old State House Museum.

Old State House

Historic facade of Old South Meeting House

6 Old South Meeting House

MAP Q3 ▪ 310 Washington St ▪ 617 482 6439 ▪ Open Apr–Oct: 9:30am–5pm daily; Nov–Mar: 10am–4pm daily ▪ Adm ▪ www. oldsouthmeetinghouse.org

Old South's rafters have rung with many impassioned speeches exhorting the overthrow of the king, the abolition of slavery, women's right to vote, an end to apartheid, and many other causes. Nearly abandoned when its congregation moved to Back Bay in 1876, it was saved in one of Boston's first acts of preservation.

7 Old Corner Bookstore

MAP P3 ▪ 1 School St

This enduring spot on the Freedom Trail remains one of the most tangible sites associated with the writers of the New England Renaissance of the last half of the 19th century. Both the *Atlantic Monthly* magazine and Ticknor & Fields (publishers of Ralph Waldo Emerson and Henry David Thoreau) made this modest structure their headquarters during the mid and late 19th century, when Boston was the literary, intellectual, and publishing center of the country.

Saving the site from demolition in 1960 led to the formation of Historic Boston Incorporated. The building, however, is no longer connected to publishing today.

8 Custom House

MAP Q3 ▪ 3 McKinley Sq ▪ 617 310 6300 ▪ Tours 2pm, 6pm Sat–Thu ▪ Adm

When the Custom House was built in 1840, Boston was one of America's largest overseas shipping ports, and customs fees were the mainstay of the Federal budget. The Neo-Classical structure once sat on the waterfront, but now stands two blocks inland. The 16-story Custom House tower, added in 1913, was Boston's first skyscraper. Since the 1990s, peregrine falcons have nested in the clock tower under the watchful eyes of wildlife biologists. Tours of the tower give views of the harbor and the skyline. A bar service is available on evening tours.

Custom House clock tower

9 Post Office Square

MAP Q3

On a sunny day this green oasis in the heart of the Financial District is filled with office workers who

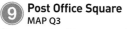

claim a bench or a spot of grass for a picnic. Surrounding the park are some of the area's most architecturally distinctive buildings, including the Art Deco post office (Congress St), the Renaissance Revival former Federal Reserve building (now the Langham, Boston hotel, see p146), and the Art Moderne New England Telephone building (185 Franklin St).

Post Office Square

10 King's Chapel
MAP P3 ∎ 58 Tremont St
∎ 617 523 1749 ∎ Open 10am–5pm Mon–Sat, 1:30–5pm Sun; call for winter hours; recitals: 12:15pm Tue ∎ Tours of crypt and bell tower: adm ∎ www.kings-chapel.org

The first Anglican Church in Puritan Boston was established in 1686 to serve British Army officers. When Anglicans fled Boston along with British forces in 1776, the chapel became the first Unitarian Church in the New World. The church is known for its program of classical concerts.

Interior of King's Chapel

See map on p100 ←

A SHOPPING SPREE

▶ MORNING

The "T" will deposit you at Downtown Crossing, where you can browse the pushcart vendors and shop the fashions and accessories of **Macy's** at leisure. Then proceed over to **DSW Shoe Warehouse** (385 Washington St) for a great selection of fashion shoes at discount prices. Make a left up Bromfield Street to peruse the fine writing implements and elegant stationery at **Bromfield Pen Shop** (5 Bromfield St). The walk to Quincy Market down Franklin Street will take you past the Financial District with its tall and imposing skyscrapers. Turn left at Post Office Square for lunch at **Sip Café** (Post Office Square Park).

AFTERNOON

Stop to enjoy a short rest outside **Quincy Market** (see p13) before you begin your spree in earnest. Numerous name-brand shops such as Victoria's Secret await. For a more local flavor try Newbury Comics (see p91), which carries a variety of Boston-themed gifts and paraphernalia. Then pay a visit to Local Charm for jewelry by local and national designers. Have an early dinner and make new friends at the communal tables at **Durgin-Park** (North Market, 617 227 2038). Order the gigantic prime rib and the Indian pudding (a cornmeal-molasses dish) for dessert. After dinner, rock out to live music at the **Hard Rock Café** (22–24 Clinton St, 617 424 7625).

Bars and Clubs

Exterior of Beantown Pub

1 Beantown Pub
MAP P3 ▪ 100 Tremont St

This no-frills tourist hangout is filled with numerous pool tables and even more TVs, all of which are tuned to big sports games and events.

2 Corner Pub
MAP G4 ▪ 162 Lincoln St

This friendly Leather District bar and grill serves excellent cocktails and a wide selection of draft beers to go with good burgers.

3 Haley.Henry Wine Bar
MAP G4 ▪ 45 Province St

This nautical-themed wine bar (see p60), housed in a chic condo building, specializes in natural wines and tinned fish from Spain and Portugal. The menu also features small plates of ceviche and crudo.

4 Stoddard's Fine Food & Ale
MAP P4 ▪ 48 Temple Pl

Handsome, retro-themed bar in the heart of the Ladder District. Beer aficionados choose from one of the area's longest lists.

5 Silvertone Bar & Grill
MAP P3 ▪ 69 Bromfield St
▪ Closed Sun

This surprisingly unpretentious, contemporary beer bar and casual restaurant is a great place for reasonably priced comfort food and drinks. The creamy mac and cheese is excellent.

6 JM Curley
MAP G4 ▪ 21 Temple Pl

Named for Boston's old-time felonious mayor, this bar has good pub victuals (served until late) and an exhaustive list of craft and mass-market beers.

7 The Tam
MAP P5 ▪ 222 Tremont St

A local favorite, The Tam is a cozy brightly lit dive bar. It serves cheap beer and generous pours of liquor. The bar accepts cash only.

8 Good Life Downtown
MAP P4 ▪ 28 Kingston St

This retro, lounge-lizard bar and club with two dance floors gets lively after work and on weekend nights. The cocktails are top notch.

9 The Merchant
MAP P4 ▪ 60 Franklin St

This spacious American brasserie is a popular late-night venue for its huge beer list, creative cocktails, and menu of savory bar bites.

10 Marliave
MAP P3 ▪ 10 Bosworth St

Opened in 1885, Marliave is one of the oldest restaurants in the city. The warmly lit bar serves creative cocktails and hosts half-price oyster happy hours daily.

Entrance to Marliave

Restaurants for Luxury Dining

PRICE CATEGORIES
For a three-course meal for one with half a bottle of wine (or equivalent meal), taxes, and extra charges.

$ under $40 $$ $40–$60 $$$ over $60

1 Yvonne's
MAP G4 ▪ 2 Winter Pl ▪ 617 267 0047 ▪ Closed L ▪ $$$

A modern twist to the concept of a supper club, Yvonne's dishes up contemporary American fare and a well-chosen collection of wines and cocktails.

Legal Crossing dining room

2 Ruth's Chris Steak House
MAP P3 ▪ 45 School St ▪ 617 742 8401 ▪ Closed L Sat & Sun ▪ $$$

Classy steak emporium located in the historic Old City Hall building. Fine service and a top-notch wine list.

3 blu
MAP P4 ▪ 4 Avery St ▪ 617 375 8550 ▪ $$$

Light, fresh, delicately nuanced, and artistically presented international cuisine is complemented by soaring Post-Modern architecture.

4 No 9 Park
MAP P3 ▪ 9 Park St ▪ 617 742 9991 ▪ $$$

Hobnob with Beacon Hill highflyers in this bold bistro overlooking Boston Common, where Mediterranean flavors meet an imaginative wine list.

5 O Ya
MAP H5 ▪ 9 East St ▪ 617 654 9900 ▪ Closed Sun & Mon ▪ $$$

One of the city's priciest and fanciest restaurants, serving modern Japanese creations close to South Station.

6 The Palm
MAP H4 ▪ 100 Oliver St ▪ 617 867 9292 ▪ $$$

The glamorous club-like setting here matches prime beef and top quality seafood with a broad wine list.

7 Legal Crossing
MAP P3 ▪ 558 Washington St ▪ 617 692 8888 ▪ $$$

Yet another popular offshoot of the iconic local Legal Sea Foods empire *(see p64)*, serving exceptionally fresh seafood, as always, along with cool, Downtown-influenced cocktails.

8 Teatro
MAP P4 ▪ 177 Tremont St ▪ 617 778 6841 ▪ Closed L ▪ No reservations ▪ $$$

A glamorous hipster scene prevails at superchef Jamie Mammano's theatrically styled trattoria, which boasts a killer wine list to go with its classic pizzas, pastas, and grills.

9 The Oceanaire Seafood Room
MAP Q3 ▪ 40 Court St ▪ 617 742 2277 ▪ $$$

This former bank retains its marble glamour in its current role as an outstanding seafood restaurant, with a superb raw bar and regional, seasonal dishes on the menu.

10 Society on High
MAP H4 ▪ 99 High St ▪ 857 350 4555 ▪ $$

Smart and contemporary, this bistro offers New England specialties, alongside a good choice of tapas and cocktails. The lobster poached in butter is heavenly.

See map on p100 ←

ᴛᴏᴘ10 Chinatown, the Theater District, and South End

Boston's compact Chinatown is one of the oldest and most significant in the US, concentrating a wealth of Asian experience in a small patch of real estate. Theater-goers find the proximity of Chinatown to the Theater District a boon for pre- and post-show dining. The Theater District itself is among the liveliest in the US, and its architecturally distinctive playhouses are nearly always active, often with local productions. Adjoining the Theater District to the south is South End, once an immigrant tenement area and now Boston's most diverse neighborhood by race, cultural background, and sexual orientation. It is also the country's largest historical district of Victorian town-houses. Following four decades of gentrification and swift inflation of real estate prices, South End is now home to a burgeoning, energetic club, café, and restaurant scene.

Tremont Street townhouse windows

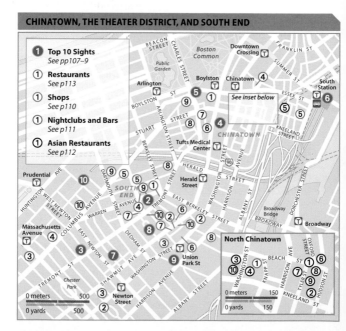

CHINATOWN, THE THEATER DISTRICT, AND SOUTH END

① **Top 10 Sights**
See pp107–9

① **Restaurants**
See p113

① **Shops**
See p110

① **Nightclubs and Bars**
See p111

① **Asian Restaurants**
See p112

Dragon Gate entrance to Chinatown on Beach Street

1 Beach Street and Chinatown

MAP P5

As the periphery of ethnic Chinatown becomes increasingly homogenized, Beach Street remains the purely Chinese heart of the neighborhood. An ornate Dragon Gate at the base of Beach Street creates a ceremonial entrance to Chinatown. The wall behind the adjacent small park is painted with a dreamy mural of a Chinese sampan boat.

2 Boston Center for the Arts

MAP F5 ■ 539 Tremont St ■ 617 426 5000 ■ www.bcaonline.org

The massive Cyclorama building is the centerpiece of the BCA, a performing and visual arts complex dedicated to nurturing new talent. The center *(see p54)* provides studio space to about 50 artists, and its Mills Gallery mounts rotating visual arts exhibitions. The BCA's four theaters host avant-garde productions of dance, theater, and performance art.

3 Tremont Street

MAP N5–M6

The part of Tremont Street between East Berkeley and Massachusetts Avenue is the social and commercial heart of the South End. Many of the handsome brick and brownstone townhouses have been restored to perfection, some with a boutique or café added at street level. The liveliest corner of the South End is the intersection of Tremont with Clarendon and Union Park streets, where the Boston Center for the Arts and a plethora of restaurants and cafés create a compact entertainment and dining district.

4 Boch Center – Wang Theatre

MAP N5 ■ 270 Tremont St ■ 617 482 9393 ■ www.bochcenter.org

With a theater modeled on the Paris Opera House and a foyer inspired by the Palace of Versailles, the opulent Wang Theatre (opened 1925) is a grand venue for touring musicals, blockbuster concerts, and local productions *(see p54)*.

Grand foyer of Wang Theatre

Piano Row
MAP N4

In the late 19th century, the head-quarters of leading piano makers Steinert, Vose, Starck, Mason & Hamlin, and Wurlitzer were all located on the section of Boylston Street facing Boston Common, giving the block (now a historic district) its nickname of Piano Row. Over a century later, those Beaux Arts buildings still echo with music. The ornate Colonial Theatre opened in 1900. It is owned and managed by Emerson College. Another attraction on Piano Row is Boylston Place, a small-scale club and nightlife center.

6 South Station
MAP Q5

A brick temple to mass transport-ation, the Neo-Classical Revival South Station was erected in 1898 at the height of rail travel in the US, and was once the country's busiest train station. Following extensive restoration in 1989, it now serves as an Amtrak terminal for trains from the south and west of the city, as well as a "T" stop and a social and commercial center with a lively food court and occasional free lunchtime concerts.

7 Villa Victoria
MAP F6 ▪ Area bounded by Shawmut Ave, Tremont St, W Newton St, & W Brookline St ▪ Center for the Arts: 85 W Newton St; 617 927 1737; www.ibaboston.org

Villa Victoria is a virtually self-contained, primarily Hispanic neighborhood that grew out of a unique collaboration among Puerto Rican community activists, flexible city planners, and visionary archi-tects. With its low-rise buildings, narrow streets, and mom-and-pop stores, Villa Victoria replicates the feel of Puerto Rican community life. At its heart, the Center for the Arts sponsors concerts and exhibitions. In mid-July the center puts on the Latino arts and cultural celebration Festival Betances.

8 Union Park
MAP F6

Constructed between 1857 and 1859, this small park surrounded by English-style brick row houses was built to contrast with the French-inspired grid layout of nearby Back Bay. Graced with lovely trees and fountains and verdant with a thick mat of grass, the square was one of the first areas in the South End to be gentrified.

South Station's imposing Neo-Classical facade

Exterior of Holy Cross Cathedral

⑨ Holy Cross Cathedral
MAP F6 ■ 1400 Washington St ■ 617 542 5682 ■ Open 9am–6pm daily

Holy Cross, the largest Roman Catholic church in Massachusetts, acts as the seat of the archbishop of Boston. The cathedral was constructed between 1866 and 1875 (on the site of the municipal gallows) to serve the largely Irish-American workers who lived in the adjoining shantytown. Today the congregation is principally of Hispanic origin. Of note are the magnificent stained-glass windows, which include rare colored glass imported from Munich in the 19th century, and the powerful Hook & Hastings organ which, when played with the stops out, seems to make every piece of Roxbury pudding-stone in the building reverberate.

⑩ Southwest Corridor Park
MAP E6

The first section of the 5-mile (8-km) Southwest Corridor Park divides South End and Back Bay along the "T" orange line corridor. In the residential South End portion, a path strings together numerous small parks. Between Massachusetts Avenue and West Roxbury, the park broadens to include amenities such as tennis and basketball courts.

EXPLORING CHINATOWN AND SOUTH END

▶ **MORNING**

Begin on **Washington Street** where you can peruse the exotic produce, Chinese teas, imported Asian spices, and specialty foods at **Jia Ho** (see p110). Continue down Essex Street, ducking into Oxford Place to see the mural, *Travelers in an Autumn Landscape*, based on the scroll painting by the same name at the Museum of Fine Arts. The distinctive and colorful **Dragon Gate** to Chinatown stands at the corner of Edinboro Street and Beach Street, along with pagoda-style phone booths. Continue to the corner of Essex and Chauncy where **Essex Corner** (see p110) offers a wide range of goods. Stop for lunch at **Shabu-Zen** (see p112)

AFTERNOON

Walk down **Tremont Street** to the South End, or hop on the "T" two stops to Back Bay Station. Head west on Columbus Avenue to see the elaborate bronze sculptures that tell the story of escaped slave Harriet Tubman, who led many others to freedom on the Underground Railroad, a series of hiding places in non-slave states. Back at Tremont Street, visit the **Boston Center for the Arts** (see p107) to get a snapshot of local contemporary art at the Mills Gallery. Then, if you have time, stroll around gracious **Union Park** before returning to the arts center for dinner and live music at **The Beehive** (see p56). There is a good chance that local jazz artists will be playing.

See map on p106 ←

Shops

1 Jia Ho Supermarket
MAP N5 ■ 692 Washington St

This compact market offers vegetables, tropical fruits, and packaged foods essential for cuisines from Singapore to Seoul.

2 Flock
MAP P6 ■ 274 Shawmut Ave ■ Closed Mon

Flock sells stylish and easy-to-wear women's clothing and accessories with a modern Bohemian flair, plus an eclectic range of gifts and afford-able home decor items.

3 Hudson
MAP F6 ■ 12 Union Park St

This home decor boutique by interior designer Jill Goldberg offers home furnishings and a delightfully eclectic mix of decorative accent pieces that includes traditional, country, vintage, and modern pieces.

4 Essex Corner
MAP P5 ■ 50 Essex St

This large shop gathers all the Asian merchandise found in Chinatown into one easy-to-peruse location.

5 Tadpole
MAP M6 ■ 58 Clarendon St

Tadpole's cheery selection of clothing, toys, and accessories for children are a favorite among the locals. Limited edition strollers are very popular.

Tadpole on Clarendon Street

Lekker Home linens

6 Lekker Home
MAP G6 ■ 1313 Washington St ■ Closed Mon

Contemporary Italian, Scandinavian, and German home design items are the highlights of this emporium, which offers the latest trends in homeware.

7 Michele Mercaldo Jewelry
MAP G6 ■ 276 Shawmut Ave ■ Closed Sun & Mon

Jewelry by contemporary designer Michele Mercaldo and her colleagues is displayed in creative and unusual ways at this South End store.

8 Bead & Fiber
MAP G6 ■ 460 Harrison Ave ■ Closed Mon

Whether you're looking for beaded jewelry or fiber art, or simply the materials to make them, this shop and gallery offers everything you need, including classes.

9 Urban Grape
MAP L4 ■ 303 Columbus Ave

This stylish award-winning liquor store uses "progressive shelving", a unique system of organizing wines by their body instead of region or variety to make it easy for customers to select wines.

10 Syrian Grocery Importing Company
MAP G5 ■ 270 Shawmut Ave ■ Closed Sun & Mon

Harking back to the South End's days as a Middle Eastern immigrant neighborhood, this grocery sells southern and eastern Mediterranean essentials, from preserved lemons to rare Moroccan argan oil.

Nightclubs and Bars

1 Whisky Saigon
MAP N5 ■ 116 Boylston St
■ 617 482 7799 ■ Closed Sun–Tue
■ Adm

The colorful and sophisticated bar up front becomes a glamorous dance scene in the back.

2 Toro
MAP F6 ■ 1704 Washington St

Barcelona-style tapas complement an all-Spanish wine list and a select group of creative cocktails with names like *Verdad y Amor* (Truth and Love).

Spanish paella at Toro

3 Wally's Café
MAP E6 ■ 427 Massachusetts Ave

Exhale before you squeeze in the door at Wally's. This thin, chock-full sliver of a room is one of the best jazz bars in Boston, and has been since 1944.

4 Five Horses Tavern
MAP F6 ■ 535 Columbus Ave
■ 617 936 3930

This atmospheric, brick-walled tavern boasts an impressive collection of craft beers from around the world. It also serves fine whiskeys and American comfort food.

5 Delux Café
MAP M6 ■ 100 Chandler St
■ Closed Sun

Cheap drinks and an Elvis shrine lend an edge to the trendy scene here. It's good clean fun for hipster grandchildren of the beatniks. Regulars and visitors alike rave about the fried chicken.

6 Royale
MAP P5 ■ 279 Tremont St
■ 617 338 7699 ■ Adm

This massive two-story dance hall occasionally morphs into a live-performance concert venue for touring acts.

7 Venu
MAP N5 ■ 100 Warrenton St
■ Closed Mon & Wed

Music varies each night of the week, but it's always the same Prada-Armani-Versace-clad crowd. The Art Deco bar makes for a beautiful look.

8 Jacque's Cabaret
MAP N5 ■ 79 Broadway ■ Adm

This multifaceted pioneer drag-queen bar features female impersonators, edgy rock bands, and cabaret shows.

9 The Beehive
MAP M6 ■ 541 Tremont St ■ 617 423 0069

Live jazz, delicious cocktails and beers, as well as good, hearty fare make The Beehive one of the best venues in South End.

10 The Butcher Shop
MAP F6 ■ 552 Tremont St

A full-service butcher shop and wine bar pairs house-made sausages, salami, and foie gras terrine with Old World wines of Italy, France, and Spain by the glass or bottle. Gourmet "Burgers and Beers" evenings take place in the summer months.

Interior of The Butcher Shop

See map on p106

Asian Restaurants

(1) Peach Farm
MAP P5 ■ 24 Tyler St
■ 617 482 3332 ■ $

Perfect for family-style dining, this restaurant lets you select your choice of fish from a tank. Good daily specials.

(2) New Shanghai
MAP H5 ■ 21 Hudson St
■ 617 338 0732 ■ $

Typical southern Chinese fare is available, but the best bets are northern dishes such as tea-smoked duck, Sichuan fish, and Mongolian beef.

Exterior of Penang

(3) Penang
MAP N5 ■ 685 Washington St
■ 617 451 6372 ■ $

Nominally "Pan-Asian," Penang has a chiefly Malay menu, ranging from inexpensive noodle staples to more contemporary concoctions.

(4) Emperor's Garden
MAP P5 ■ 690 Washington St
■ 617 482 8898 ■ $

Dim sum in this historical opera house is a theatrical experience. Note that most southern Chinese dishes are large and best shared.

(5) Hei La Moon
MAP Q5 ■ 88 Beach St ■ 617 338 8813 ■ $

A huge, rather formal Pan-Chinese restaurant on the Leather District side of Atlantic Avenue. On weekend mornings, a large crowd is guaranteed for the dim sum.

(6) Taiwan Cafe
MAP P5 ■ 34 Oxford St
■ 617 426 8181 ■ No credit cards
■ $

The typically Taiwanese over-bright cafeteria appearance of this place should not deter aficionados of authentic, adventurous dishes like spicy pig ears and jellyfish.

(7) Shojo
MAP P5 ■ 9A Tyler St ■ 617 423 7888 ■ $$

Savor suckling pig *bao* (steamed stuffed bun) and chicken tacos with *yuzu* slaw at this snazzy Japanese restaurant. Superb craft cocktails.

(8) China King
MAP P5 ■ 60 Beach St ■ 617 542 1763 ■ $

This eatery offers an extensive menu of Chinese delicacies, plus the must-try Peking duck. Order it a day ahead for a minimum of four diners.

(9) Shabu-Zen
MAP P5 ■ 16 Tyler St ■ 617 292 8828 ■ $$

Choose your meats and vegetables and your cooking liquid at this traditional Asian "hot-pot" joint.

(10) Dumpling Café
MAP G5 ■ 695 Washington St
■ 617 338 8858 ■ $

This casual spot sells several varieties of dumpling made fresh daily, alongside delicacies such as duck tongue.

Diners at Dumpling Café

Restaurants

PRICE CATEGORIES

For a three-course meal for one with half
a bottle of wine (or equivalent meal),
taxes, and extra charges.

$ under $40 $$ $40–$60 $$$ over $60

1 Picco
MAP F5 ■ 513 Tremont St
■ 617 927 0066 ■ $

This friendly little place is popular for
its thin-crust, wood-fired pizzas and
decadent homemade ice cream.

2 Myers + Chang
MAP G6 ■ 1145 Washington St
■ 617 542 5200 ■ $$

Clever reinventions of classic
Chinese dishes such as lemon
shrimp dumplings are served here.
Wash down with sake-based cock-
tails containing guava and lychee.

3 El Centro
MAP F6 ■ 472 Shawmut Ave
■ 617 262 5708 ■ $

Authentic Mexican cuisine from
a Sonoran chef emphasizes fresh
flavors and serves authentic tamales
and tortillas made from scratch.

4 Banyan Bar + Refuge
MAP F6 ■ 553 Tremont St
■ 617 556 4211 ■ $$

A chic Pan-Asian gastropub, Banyan
Bar + Refuge serves innovative fare
such as roasted chicken with wasabi
gratin potatoes and kimchi fried rice.

5 Les Zygomates
MAP Q5 ■ 129 South St ■ 617
541 5108 ■ Closed Sun ■ $$$

French bistro fare, dozens of wines
by the glass, and live jazz is on offer
near Boston South Station.

6 Coppa
MAP F6 ■ 252 Shawmut Ave
■ 617 391 0902 ■ Closed L Sat ■ $

Small, Italian-inspired plates make
Coppa perfect for grazing while
sipping glasses of wine and basking
in the romantic ambience.

Aquitaine's classically French interior

7 Aquitaine
MAP F5 ■ 569 Tremont St ■ 617
424 8577 ■ Closed L Mon–Fri ■ $$$

A Parisian-style bistro popular for
its snazzy wine bar and its French
market-style cooking. Black truffle
vinaigrette makes Aquitaine's steak-
frites Boston's best.

8 Masa
MAP N6 ■ 439 Tremont St
■ 617 338 8884 ■ Closed L ■ $$$

Refined New American dishes
with southwestern accents are
complemented by killer margaritas,
colorful decor, and good wines.

9 Ostra
MAP N5 ■ 1 Charles St S
■ 617 421 1200 ■ $$$

This sophisticated restaurant in the
Theater District serves contemporary
Mediterranean fare in both innovative
and classic preparations.

10 Giacomo's
MAP L6 ■ 431 Columbus Ave
■ 617 536 5723 ■ $

This offshoot of a very popular North
End eatery offers heaped portions of
filling Italian fare at great prices. The
restaurant accepts cash only.

See map on p106 ←

🔟 Kenmore and the Fenway

On days when the Red Sox are playing a home baseball game at Fenway Park, Kenmore Square is packed with fans. By night, Kenmore becomes the jump-off point for a night of dancing, drinking, and socializing at clubs on or near Lansdowne Street. Yet for all of Kenmore's genial rowdiness, it is also the gateway into the sedate parkland of the Back Bay Fens and the stately late 19th- and early 20th-century buildings along the Fenway. The Fenway neighborhood extends all the way southeast to

Huntington Avenue, aka the "Avenue of the Arts," which links key cultural centers such as Symphony Hall, Huntington Theatre, the Museum of Fine Arts, Massachusetts College of Art and Design, and the delightful and not-to-be-missed Isabella Stewart Gardner Museum along a tree-lined boulevard.

Entrance to the Back Bay Fens

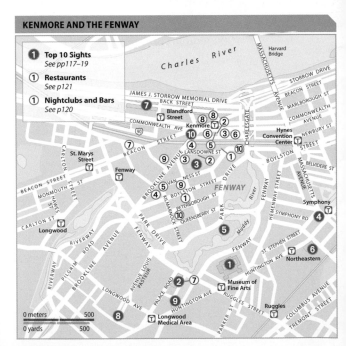

KENMORE AND THE FENWAY

① **Top 10 Sights**
See pp117–19

① **Restaurants**
See p121

① **Nightclubs and Bars**
See p120

1 Museum of Fine Arts

One of the most largest fine arts museums in the country, the MFA is especially renowned for its collections of French Impressionism and of ancient Egyptian and Nubian art and artifacts. Its Asian art holdings are said to be the largest in the United States (see pp28–31).

2 Isabella Stewart Gardner Museum

This Fenway museum, in a faux Venetian palace, represents the exquisite personal tastes of its founder, Isabella Stewart Gardner, who was one of the country's premier art collectors at the end of the 19th century (see pp34–5).

3 Fenway Park

MAP D5 ▪ 4 Jersey St ▪ 617 267 1700 for tickets, 617 226 6666 for tours ▪ Tours year-round: 9am–5pm daily (from 10am in winter; last tour 3 hours before game time) ▪ Adm ▪ www.redsox.com

Built in 1912, the home field of the Boston Red Sox is the oldest surviving park in major league baseball, and aficionados insist that it's also the finest. An odd-shaped parcel of land gives the park quirky features, such as the high, green-painted wall in left field, affectionately known as "the Green Monster." Although previous owners threatened to abandon Fenway, the current ones have enlarged the park to accommodate more loyal Sox fans. Behind-the-scenes tours include areas normally closed to the public, like the dugouts and private boxes.

Performance at Symphony Hall

4 Symphony Hall

MAP E6 ▪ 301 Massachusetts Ave ▪ 617 266 1492 ▪ www.bso.org

The restrained, elegant Italian Renaissance exterior of this 1900 concert hall barely hints at what is considered to be the acoustic perfection of the interior hall. Home of the Boston Symphony Orchestra, the hall's 2,300-plus seats are usually sold out for their classical concerts, as well as for the lighter Boston Pops (see p54).

5 Back Bay Fens

MAP D5–D6 ▪ Bounded by Park Dr & The Fenway

This lush ribbon of grassland, marshes, and stream banks follows Muddy River and forms one link in the Emerald Necklace of parks (see p19). The enclosed James P. Kelleher Rose Garden in the center of the Fens offers a perfect spot for quiet contemplation. A path runs from Kenmore Square to the museums and galleries on Huntington Avenue, which makes a pleasant shortcut through the Fens. Best by daylight.

Fenway Park baseball park

Magnificent interior of Jordan Hall

6 Jordan Hall

This concert hall at the New England Conservatory of Music opened in 1903 and underwent an $8.2 million restoration in 1995. Musicians often praise its acoustics, heralding Jordan as "the Stradivarius of concert halls." Hundreds of free classical concerts are performed at this National Historic Landmark hall every year (see p55).

A play at Boston Playwrights' Theatre

7 Boston University

■ Howard Gotlieb Archival Research Center; MAP C4; 771 Commonwealth Ave; 617 353 3696; exhibit rooms open 9am–4pm Mon–Fri; adm ■ Boston Playwrights' Theatre; MAP C5; 949 Commonwealth Ave; 866 811 4111; season runs Oct–Apr ■ www.bu.edu

Founded as a Methodist Seminary in 1839, Boston University was chartered as a university in 1869. Today it enrolls approximately 30,000 students from all 50 states and some 125 countries. The scattered colleges and schools were consolidated at the Charles River Campus in 1966. Both sides of Commonwealth Avenue are lined with distinctive university buildings and sculptures. The Howard Gotlieb Archival Research Center is big on the memorabilia of show business figures, displayed on a rotating basis. Artifacts include Gene Kelly's Oscar and a number of Bette Davis's film scripts. It also exhibits selections from its holdings of rare manuscripts and books. The Boston Playwrights' Theatre was founded by the late Nobel Laureate Derek Walcott in 1981 to help develop new plays. A season highlight is the day-long Boston Theater Marathon of 50 ten-minute plays.

8 Warren Anatomical Museum

MAP C6 ■ 10 Shattuck St ■ 617 432 6196 ■ Open 9am–5pm Mon–Fri

Established in 1847 from the private holdings of Dr. John Collins Warren, this museum contains the former anatomical teaching collections of the Harvard Medical School, including clinical examples of rare deformities and diseases. Among the excellent displays are several delicate and poignant skeletons of stillborn conjoined twins. The unusual collections are still used for medical education.

9 Massachusetts College of Art and Design Galleries

MAP D6 ■ 621 Huntington Ave ■ 617 879 7337 ■ Closed for renovation until 2020 ■ www.massart.edu

The Paine and Bakalar galleries in the South Building of the Massachusetts College of Art and Design mount some of Boston's most dynamic exhibitions of contemporary visual art. It is the only independent state-supported art college in the US and exhibitions tend to emphasize avant-garde experimentation as well as social commentary and documentary.

10 Kenmore Square

MAP D5

Largely dominated by Boston University, Kenmore Square is now being transformed from a student ghetto into an extension of upmarket Back Bay, losing some of its funky character but gaining élan in the process. As the public transportation gateway to Fenway Park, the square swarms with baseball fans and sidewalk vendors, rather than students, on game days. The most prominent landmark of the square is the CITGO sign, its more than 9,000 ft (2,743 m) of LEDs pulsing red, white, and blue from dusk until midnight. *Time* magazine designated this sign an "objet d'heart" because it was so beloved by Bostonians that they prevented its dismantling in 1983.

Kenmore Square, with its CITGO sign

A DAY OF THE ARTS

Howard Gotlieb Archival Research Center
Kenmore Square
Boston University Central Station
Fenway Park
Lucky Strike Social
Back Bay Fens
Isabella Stewart Gardner Museum, Café G
Museum of Fine Arts
Jordan Hall

▶ MORNING AND AFTERNOON

Take the green line "T" (B train) to Boston University Central and make your way to the **Howard Gotlieb Archival Research Center**, part of **Boston University**, for a glimpse of show business ephemera, including Fred Astaire's dance shoes. Then head west toward **Kenmore Square** to explore the stores, including the encyclopedic Boston University Bookstore *(660 Beacon St)*, directly under the CITGO sign. Stroll along Brookline Avenue to **Fenway Park** for a tour of the stadium *(see p117)* and then take Jersey Street to the **Back Bay Fens** *(see p117)*, where you can rest beneath the wings of the angel on the Veteran's Memorial. Continue to the **Museum of Fine Arts** *(see pp28–31)* to view the outstanding art collections – from ancient Egyptian artifacts to contemporary installations. Afterward, follow the Fenway three blocks left to continue your immersion in art at the **Isabella Stewart Gardner Museum** *(see pp34–5)*. Take a break in the "living room" of the museum's Renzo Piano-designed wing, then grab a bite to eat at the classy **Café G** *(see p121)*.

EVENING

You can pack in a full evening of entertainment by taking in a recital at **Jordan Hall** *(see p55)*. When the final applause has died down, make your way to **Lucky Strike Social** *(see p120)* and round off the night with billiards, bowling, and video games. You may want to continue into the early hours.

See map on p116

Nightclubs and Bars

 Loretta's Last Call
MAP D5 ▪ 1 Lansdowne St

Country music and Southern food fuel this happening bar and dance club. The interior has a cozy, vintage ambience.

 Bleacher Bar
MAP D5 ▪ 82A Lansdowne St

This tiny bar, tucked in the back of Fenway Park, has several seats offering direct views into the venue. Inviting pub fare and a well-stocked bar keep customers occupied.

 Audubon Boston
MAP D5 ▪ 836 Beacon St

Close enough to Fenway Park to drop by after the game, Audubon Boston is a relaxed neighborhood bar and grill with good food, beer, and a thoughtful wine list.

4 **Cask 'n Flagon**
MAP D5 ▪ 62 Brookline Ave
▪ Closed Sun

At Fenway's premier sports bar, fans hoist a cold one and debate the merits of the Sox manager's latest tactics.

5 **Hawthorne**
MAP D5 ▪ Hotel Commonwealth, 500 Commonwealth Ave

Cocktails and champagnes star in this upscale lounge for Kenmore Square adults who would rather converse than yell.

Game On! sports bar

6 **Game On!**
MAP D5 ▪ 82 Lansdowne St

Wall-to-wall TVs are tuned to every game that's on anywhere in the country at this bar in a corner of Fenway Park. A prime spot for sports fans to eat, drink, and cheer.

7 **Lower Depths Tap Room**
MAP D5 ▪ 476 Commonwealth Ave

This underground bar in Kenmore Square features tater tots and beer cheese dip on the menu, plus an extensive list of local craft brews. There are good options for retro drinkers, such as the Genesse Cream Ale. The bar accepts cash only.

8 **Cornwall's Pub**
MAP D5 ▪ 654 Beacon St

Offering the very best of both worlds, Cornwall's is a British-style pub with a wide range of good beers, ales, and food, but the bartenders also understand baseball.

9 **Boston Beer Works**
MAP D5 ▪ 61 Brookline Ave

This cavernous brew pub specializes in lighter American ales and serves giant plates of ribs and chicken that can easily feed two ravenous Red Sox fans.

10 **Lucky Strike Social**
MAP D5 ▪ 145 Ipswich St

Set behind Fenway Park, this entertainment complex features bowling lanes, pool tables, and video games, as well as the popular brewpub, Cheeky Monkey.

Elegant Hawthorne lounge-bar

Restaurants

 Citizen Public House
MAP E5 ▪ 1310 Boylston St
▪ 617 450 9000 ▪ $$

Craft beers, 100 whiskeys, excellent cocktails, and great pub food make Citizen a top neighborhood spot.

2 **Island Creek Oyster Bar**
MAP D5 ▪ 500 Commonwealth Ave ▪ 617 532 5300 ▪ Closed L Mon–Fri ▪ $$$

Owned by the Duxbury oyster farm of the same name, this swanky room excels at great local seafood with outstanding wines.

3 **India Quality**
MAP D4 ▪ 484 Commonwealth Ave ▪ 617 267 4499 ▪ $

Long-time favorite of Boston University students, India Quality focuses on northern Indian dishes roasted in a tandoor oven, but serves up several excellent fish and spicy plates as well.

Interior of Sweet Cheeks

4 **Sweet Cheeks**
MAP E5 ▪ 1381 Boylston St
▪ 617 266 1300 ▪ $$

Chef-owner Tiffani Faison is crazy about authentic Southern barbecue. Order pork belly by the pound and drink sweet tea from Mason jars.

PRICE CATEGORIES
For a three-course meal for one with half a bottle of wine (or equivalent meal), taxes and extra charges.

$ under $40 $$ $40–$60 $$$ over $60

5 **Wahlburgers**
MAP D5 ▪ 132 Brookline Ave
▪ 617 927 6810 ▪ $

Chef Paul, brother of actor Mark Walhberg, runs this tongue-in-cheek joint that serves burgers with a twist.

6 **Eastern Standard**
MAP D5 ▪ 528 Commonwealth Ave ▪ 617 532 9100 ▪ $$$

Buttoned-down versions of continental classics have some hidden surprises on this menu, such as magnificent salt-cod fritters and Boston cream pie.

7 **Café G**
MAP D6 ▪ 25 Evans Way
▪ 617 566 1088 ▪ Closed D, Mon ▪ $

Superb light fare, rich desserts, and fine wines complete a visit to the Isabella Stewart Gardner Museum (see pp.34–5).

8 **UBurger**
MAP D5 ▪ 636 Beacon St
▪ 617 536 0448 ▪ $

What a concept – fast food, but made to order, and just as you like it. With over two dozen toppings you can truly customize your burger.

9 **Tasty Burger**
MAP D5 ▪ 1301 Boylston St
▪ 617 425 4444 ▪ $

This no-frills burger joint in the shadow of Fenway Park offers a variety of toppings and a wide assortment of beer.

10 **El Pelon Taqueria**
MAP D5 ▪ 92 Peterborough St
▪ 617 262 9090 ▪ $

A charming little eatery that churns out tasty Mexican-American treats at very competitive prices.

See map on p116 ←

TOP 10 Cambridge and Somerville

Harvard may be Cambridge's undeniable claim to worldwide fame, but that is not to diminish the city's vibrant neighborhoods, superb restaurants, unique shops, and colorful bars lying just beyond the school's gates. Harvard Square, with its international newsstands, name-brand shopping, and numerous coffeehouses, is a heady mix of urban bohemia and Main Street USA. To the northwest, the heavily residential city of Somerville has become a magnet for young artists, musicians, and social media practitioners. Quirky shops and bars fill its squares.

Peabody Museum exhibit

CAMBRIDGE AND SOMERVILLE

1 Harvard University

While its stellar reputation might suggest visions of ivory towers in the sky, Harvard is a surprisingly accessible, welcoming place. Still, too often, visitors limit themselves to what is visible from the Yard: Massachusetts Hall, the Widener Library, maybe University Hall. But with other buildings by Gropius and Le Corbusier, top-notch museums, the eclectic Harvard Square, and performing arts spaces such as the Loeb Drama Center and Memorial Hall's Sanders Theatre *(see p55)* lying just beyond the Yard, Harvard provides every incentive to linger a while *(see pp20–23)*.

2 Harvard Art Museums
MAP B1 ▪ 32 Quincy St ▪ 617 495 9400 ▪ Open 10am–5pm daily ▪ Adm ▪ www.harvard artmuseums.org

Harvard has some of the world's finest collegiate art collections. The Fogg, Sackler, and Busch-Reisinger museums, which make up the Harvard Art Museums *(see p23)*, share space in a Renzo Piano-designed facility. Visitors will enjoy the surprising juxtapositions of Chinese bronzes, Greek vases, medieval altarpieces, and German Expressionist paintings with a visit to all three museums.

Natural History Museum

3 Peabody and Natural History Museums
Peabody Museum: MAP B1; 11 Divinity Ave; 617 496 1027; open 9am–5pm daily; adm ▪ Museum of Natural History: MAP B1; 26 Oxford St; 617 495 3045; open 9am–5pm daily; adm ▪ www.hmsc.harvard.edu

Its ongoing commitment to research aside, the Peabody Museum excels at illustrating how interactions between distinct cultures have affected peoples' lives and livelihoods *(see p21)*. Its North American Indian exhibit displays artifacts that reflect the aftermath of encounters between white Europeans and Native Americans. The Museum of Natural History delves even deeper in time, exhibiting eons-old natural wonders *(see p20)*.

1 Top 10 Sights
See pp123–5

① **Restaurants**
See p129

① **Offbeat Shops**
See p126

① **Nightclubs and Bars**
See p128

① **Places to Mix with the Locals**
See p127

4 Charles Riverbanks
MAP B2–F3

Whether you're cheering the rowers of the Head of the Charles Regatta (see p73) or watching the "T" cross Longfellow Bridge through a barrage of snowflakes, the banks of the Charles River offer a fantastic vantage point for taking in Boston's celebrated scenes. On summer Sundays, the adjacent Memorial Drive becomes a sea of strollers, joggers, and rollerbladers (see p127).

5 Multicultural Arts Center
MAP F2 ■ 41 2nd St ■ 617 577 1400 ■ Open 10:30am–6pm Mon–Fri

Housed in a beautiful 19th-century courthouse, the MAC presents a range of performance and visual art exhibitions which promote cross-cultural exchange, including summer programs in local parks. A unique feature is the encouragement of dialogue between audience and artist after performances and openings.

Multicultural Arts Center

6 Inman Square
MAP D1

Often overlooked, Inman Square is possibly Cambridge's best-kept secret. Home to popular restaurants and cafés such as S&S Deli and 1369 Coffee House (see p127), the hip Bukowski Tavern, plus Christina's delectable ice creams (see p67), Inman rewards those who are willing to go out of their way to experience a real-deal Cambridge neighborhood.

Somerville Theatre, Davis Square

7 Davis Square

With its cooler-than-thou coffee shops, lively bar scene, affordable restaurants, and the renowned Somerville Theatre (see p54), Davis Square, Somerville, stands as the area's most desirable neighborhood for many young Bostonians. And with prestigious Tufts University a 10-minute walk away, the square's youthful spirit is in a constant state of replenishment.

8 Longfellow House
MAP A1 ■ 105 Brattle St ■ 617 876 4491 ■ Open Jun–Oct; tours 9:30am–5pm Wed–Sun ■ www.nps.gov/long

Poet Henry Wadsworth Longfellow can be credited with helping to shape Boston's – and America's – collective identity. His poetic documentation of Paul Revere's midnight ride (see p44) immortalized both him and his subject. In 1837, Longfellow took up residence in this house, a few blocks from Harvard Yard. He was not the first illustrious resident of this house. General George Washington headquartered

---

LOCAL STAGES

The performing arts form part of the character of Cambridge and Somerville. The ornate Somerville Theatre (see p54) draws nationally recognized musical acts, while the Loeb Drama Center (64 Brattle Street, 617 547 8300) stages The American Repertory Theater's daring, top-notch productions. And Harvard student-produced pieces grace the Hasty Pudding Theater's stage (12 Holyoke St, Cambridge, 617 495 5205).

and planned the 1776 siege of Boston in these rooms. The building is preserved with furnishings of Longfellow's family life, and houses the poet's archives.

9 Museum of Science

MAP N1 ■ Science Park ■ 617 723 2500 ■ Open 9am–5pm Mon–Thu, Sat & Sun (Jul–Sep: to 7pm), 9am–9pm Fri ■ Adm ■ www.mos.org

Exploring the cosmos in the Hayden Planetarium, hitting the high notes on a musical staircase, experiencing larger-than-life IMAX films in the Mugar Omni Theater – the Museum of Science certainly knows how to make learning enjoyable. In addition to these attractions, the museum hosts blockbuster shows like Harry Potter: The Exhibit. Live presentations take place throughout the day.

Massachusetts Institute of Technology

10 Massachusetts Institute of Technology (MIT)

MAP D3 ■ 77 Massachusetts Ave ■ 617 253 4795 ■ List Visual Arts Center: 20 Ames St, Cambridge ■ 617 253 4680 ■ Open noon–6pm Tue–Sun (to 8pm Thu) ■ MIT Museum: 265 Massachusetts Ave; 617 253 5927; open 10am–5pm daily (to 6pm Jul–Aug); adm ■ www.mit.edu

MIT has been the country's leading technical university since its founding in 1861. Its List Visual Arts Center exhibits work that comments on technology or employs it in fresh, surprising ways. Also of note is the MIT Museum, with its interactive exhibits on such fascinating topics as artificial intelligence, holography, and the world's first computers.

THE CAMBRIDGE CURRICULUM

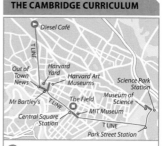

▶ MORNING

Begin your morning with a cup of gourmet coffee and light breakfast at the popular **Diesel Café** on Davis Square. Next, ride the "T" inbound to Harvard and head straight to **Out of Town News** *(0 Harvard Sq)* to peruse the mind-boggling selection of international newspapers and magazines. Visit **Harvard Yard** *(see p20)* and the John Harvard Statue and then walk east to Quincy Street and north to the **Harvard Art Museums** *(see p123)*. Walk south to Massachusetts Avenue, and turn right to legendary **Mr Bartley's** *(1246 Massachusetts Ave)* for a lunch of speciality burgers and sweet potato fries.

AFTERNOON

Ride the "T" inbound to Central Square, and walk southeast along Massachusetts Avenue to the **MIT Museum**, where exhibits of scientific, artistic and technological innovations reflect the creative energy of MIT. Return to Central Square and ride the "T" to Park Street. Then ride the Green Line "T" to Science Park and the **Museum of Science**. In this museum you can choose from 700 interactive exhibits, take a virtual tour of Acadia National Park, which showcases a specimen of every bird found in New England, learn about nanotechnology, and explore the biology of human life. Then retrace your route on the "T" to Central Square, where you can sit back and enjoy a refreshing glass of Guinness in the convivial atmosphere at **The Field** *(20 Prospect St)*.

See map on pp122–3 ←

Offbeat Shops

1 Black Ink
MAP B1 ▪ 5 Brattle St,
Cambridge

From aluminum ring binders to
spring-clip photo frames, Black Ink
features quirky items you didn't
know you couldn't live without.

2 Magpie
416 Highland Ave, Somerville

Packed with handmade crafts,
art by local artists, and goods
from indie designers, this
hipster Davis Square
boutique playfully
advertises "shiny
things for your nest."

3 Ward Maps
1735
Massachusetts Ave,
Cambridge ▪ Closed Mon

**Bags of seeds
from Magpie**

In addition to some utterly lovely
antique map reproductions, this
shop stocks MBTA-themed items
such as mugs, key chains, tote
bags and toy trains and buses.

4 Abodeon
1731 Massachusetts Ave,
Cambridge ▪ Closed Mon & Tue

Abodeon stocks an eclectic mix
of modern and vintage home
furnishings, bath and beauty
products, jewelry, lighting fixtures,
and other clever accessories.

5 Hubba Hubba
MAP C2 ▪ 2 Ellery St,
Cambridge ▪ Closed Sun

If Cambridge's Puritanical founders
could see it now... fetishist accessories, spiked belts, leather corsets,
and not-so-innocent toys line the
shelves of this risqué boutique.

6 The Million Year Picnic
MAP A1 ▪ 99 Mt Auburn St,
Cambridge

New England's oldest comic
bookstore keeps its faithful
customers happy with an
extensive back-issue selection,
graphic novels, rare imports, and
all the latest indie comics, along
with toys and T-shirts.

7 Oona's Experienced Clothing
MAP B2 ▪ 1210 Massachusetts
Ave, Cambridge

This secondhand store has been
stocking vintage as well as modern
clothes since 1972.

8 Games People Play
MAP B1 ▪ 1100 Massachusetts
Ave, Cambridge

Board games, card games,
role-playing games, word
games, action games,
puzzles... if someone
plays it, Games People Play
either sells it or can order
it in for you in a couple of days.

9 Cardullo's Gourmet Shoppe
MAP B1 ▪ 6 Brattle St, Cambridge

Harvard Square's oldest culinary
store specializes in gourmet foods
and beverages from around the
world. You can also buy made-to-
order deli sandwiches for lunch.

Exterior of Cardullo's

10 Porter Exchange Mall
1815 Massachusetts Ave,
Cambridge

Take a trip to Asia in this renovated
1928 Art Deco building, housing
a Japanese-style noodle hall and a
gift shop with all sorts of wonderful
Far Eastern ephemera.

See map on pp122–3

Places to Mix with the Locals

Memorial Drive in the fall

1 Memorial Drive
MAP B4–F3

Memorial Drive is a magnet for joggers and rollerbladers. On summer Sundays, the road closes to vehicular traffic and becomes the city's best people-watching spot.

2 The Pit
MAP B1 ■ Bounded by JFK St & Massachusetts Ave, Cambridge

On and around this sunken brick platform, street musicians, protesters, punk rockers, and uncategorizables create a scene worthy of a *Life* magazine spread.

3 The Neighborhood
MAP D1 ■ 25 Bow St, Somerville ■ 617 623 9710 ■ $

Sunday brunch at the Neighborhood brings throngs intent on securing seating beneath the outdoor grape arbors. Equally coveted are the Portuguese breakfast bread platters.

4 1369 Coffee House
MAP D1 ■ 1369 Cambridge St, Cambridge ■ 617 576 1369 ■ $

Set on Inman Square, this branch of 1369 has poetry readings, mellow music, and courteous staff, which give it a neighborly atmosphere.

5 Brattle Theatre
■ MAP B1 ■ 40 Brattle St, Cambridge ■ 617 876 6837

A Harvard Square institution, the Brattle screens cinema greats daily. Visiting on a rainy afternoon? Take in a 2-for-1 Fellini double feature for under $15.

6 Cambridge Public Library
MAP C2 ■ 449 Broadway, Cambridge ■ 617 349 4040

Families with children, dog-owners tending to canine playgroups, and locals cover the lawns in warm weather. Indoors, folks stretch out in armchairs with a book and free Wi-fi.

7 Improv Boston
MAP C2 ■ 40 Prospect St, Cambridge ■ 617 576 1253

The improvisational comedy troupe here will often explore the offbeat side of Boston life and welcomes audience participation.

8 Club Passim
MAP B1 ■ 47 Palmer St, Cambridge ■ 617 492 7679

The subterranean epicenter of New England's thriving folk music scene regularly welcomes nationally renowned artists. It also has an on-site restaurant, The Kitchen, which serves dinner and Sunday brunch.

9 Trum Ball Fields
Broadway, Somerville

Summer in Somerville is epitomized by one thing: baseball at the playground. On most weeknights, you can watch energetic youngsters take their swings.

10 Dado Tea
MAP B1 ■ 50 Church St, Cambridge ■ 617 547 0950

This Harvard Square hangout, owned by locals, is a serene, tranquil place to settle in with a cup of exotic tea and healthy pastries, sandwiches, wraps, and salads.

Nightclubs and Bars

The Middle East live music club

1 The Middle East
MAP D3 ■ 472–480 Massachusetts Ave, Cambridge ■ 617 864 3278 ■ Adm

A live music club to rival any in New York or Los Angeles, the Middle East rocks its patrons from three stages and nourishes them with delicious kebabs and curries.

2 Sinclair
MAP B1 ■ 52 Church St

Harvard Square's primary live gig venue attracts a wide assortment of acts. The front room doubles as a trendy restaurant and lounge, and it's open into the small hours every night of the week.

3 Regattabar
MAP B2 ■ 1 Bennett St, Cambridge ■ Closed Sun & Mon

Befitting its location in the sleek Charles Hotel, Regattabar offers a refined yet casual setting for watching jazz giants. Shows sell out quickly.

4 The Burren
247 Elm St, Somerville ■ 617 776 6896

This friendly Irish bar features live music almost every night, and the performances range from Irish sessions to bluegrass to swing and jazz. The backroom has comedy, step-dancing, and a weekly open mic.

5 Trina's Starlite Lounge
MAP D1 ■ 3 Beacon St, Somerville

A relaxed vibe, cheap beer, and diner-style food such as chicken-and-waffles and Sloppy Joes makes Trina's the preferred hangout for a generation of Somerville-Cambridge hipsters.

6 Hong Kong
MAP B2 ■ 1238 Massachusetts Ave, Cambridge ■ Comedy club closed Mon

Chinese food at ground level gives way to a bustling lounge on the second floor and a raucous comedy nightclub on the third. Tuesday night features a comic magic show.

7 Lord Hobo
MAP D ■ 292 Hampshire St, Cambridge

Forty draft beers, homey bistro food, and an inventive cocktail program attract an eclectic crowd, from hipsters to software geeks.

8 Lizard Lounge
MAP B1 ■ 1667 Massachusetts Ave, Cambridge

Just outside Harvard Square, the Lizard Lounge attracts a young, alternative rock- and folk-loving crowd with the promise of good live music and a small cover charge.

9 The Cantab Lounge
MAP C2 ■ 738 Massachusetts Ave, Cambridge

Live local rock performances, poetry slams, open mic nights, and other such events light up the small but lively stage at this blue-collar beer bar in Central Square.

10 Beat Brew Hall
MAP B1 ■ 13 Brattle St, Cambridge

Beat is a modern beer hall that serves over 24 beers on draft, craft cocktails, and delicious pub fare in a convivial setting. The bar features communal tables and live music.

Restaurants

PRICE CATEGORIES
For a three-course meal for one with half
a bottle of wine (or equivalent meal),
taxes, and extra charges.
....
$ under $40 $$ $40–$60 $$$ over $60

1 Oleana
MAP D2 ■ 134 Hampshire St,
Cambridge ■ 617 661 0505 ■ Closed L
daily ■ $$$

Chef Ana Sortun's mastery of spices
is evident in Oleana's sumptuous
Middle Eastern cuisine, served in a
casually elegant dining room and
a pretty courtyard with a fountain.

2 The Kirkland Tap & Trotter
MAP C1 ■ 425 Washington St
■ 857 259 6585 ■ $$$

Chef Tony Maws of Craigie on Main
fame showcases his simpler, yet
creative, home-style dishes in casual
environs. Try the unique cocktails.

Bar at the Kirkland Tap & Trotter

3 Craigie On Main
MAP D3 ■ 853 Main St,
Cambridge ■ 617 497 5511 ■ $$$

"Nose-to-tail" fine dining is the style
at Tony Maw's main venue. The menu
changes daily, and includes six- and
eight-course tasting versions.

4 Posto
MAP B2 ■ 187 Elm St,
Somerville ■ 617 625 0600 ■ Closed
L Mon–Sat ■ $

Handmade pastas, Naples-certified
pizza, and wood-grilled meats and
fish make Posto one of the most
popular restaurants in Davis Square.

5 Catalyst
MAP E3 ■ 300 Technology Sq,
Cambridge ■ 617 576 3000 ■ $$

This elegant restaurant serves
innovative locavore dishes. Craft
beers attract the coders while good
wines soothe the biotech execs.
Its summer patio is a real plus.

6 Redbones
55 Chester St, Somerville
■ 617 628 2200 ■ $$

Redbones' kitchen creates some
of the best barbecue north of the
Carolinas, and the atmosphere is
emphatically Southern.

7 Viale
MAP C3 ■ 502 Massachusetts
Ave, Cambridge ■ 617 576 1900
■ Closed L daily ■ $$$

Delightful Mediterranean dishes
and innovative cocktails make this
friendly bar-restaurant a go-to
place for food and drinks.

8 Area 4
MAP D2 ■ 500 Technology Sq,
Cambridge ■ 617 758 4444 ■ $

Food is served as early as 7am at
this bakery-café, and continues
into the night with New American
comfort food and pizzas.

9 Puritan & Company
MAP D2 ■ 1166 Cambridge St,
Cambridge ■ 617 876 0286 ■ Closed L
Mon–Sat ■ $$$

Excellent farm-to-table dining venue
that re-invents New England cuisine
with dishes such as seared scallops
with tomatillos. Sunday brunch is
a major foodie scene.

10 Harvest
MAP B1 ■ 44 Brattle St,
Cambridge ■ 617 868 2255 ■ $$$

A local institution, Harvest (see p63)
serves delicious contemporary
dishes, all prepared with fresh
seasonal ingredients. The restaurant is known for its superb
three-course Sunday brunch.

See map on pp122–3

🔟 South of Boston

South of Fort Point Channel, Boston's neighborhoods of Jamaica Plain, Roxbury, Dorchester, and South Boston are a mixture of densely residential streets and leafy parklands that form part of Frederick Law Olmsted's Emerald Necklace *(see p19)*. The lively street scenes of Boston's African-American, Latin-American, and Irish-American communities make the city's southerly neighborhoods a dynamic ethnic contrast to the more homogenized city core. Often ignored by tourists, the area south of Boston is full of quirky shops, local bars, hot nightclubs, and great off-beat places to enjoy ethnic food. This area is a little harder to reach but it is worth the effort to experience a more diverse Boston.

Forest Hills Cemetery in Fall

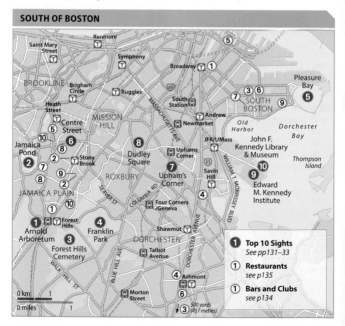

SOUTH OF BOSTON

- **1** Top 10 Sights
  See pp131–33
- **1** Restaurants
  see p135
- **1** Bars and Clubs
  see p134

Arnold Arboretum

1 Arnold Arboretum
125 Arborway, Jamaica Plain
■ 617 524 1718

One of the US's foremost collections of temperate-zone trees and shrubs covers the peaceful 0.4-sq-mile- (1.1-sq-km-) arboretum. Grouped in scientific fashion, they are a favorite subject for landscape painters, and a popular resource for botanists and gardeners. The world's most extensive lilac collection blooms from early May through late June, and thousands of Bostonians turn out for Lilac Sunday, in mid-May, to picnic and enjoy the peak of the Syringa blooms. The main flowering period of mountain laurel, azaleas, and other rhododendrons begins around Memorial Day (at the end of May).

2 Jamaica Pond
Jamaica Pond Boathouse, Jamaica Way ■ 617 522 5061
■ Open May–Oct: 10am–sunset daily
■ www.cityofboston.gov/parks

This appealing large pond and its surrounding leafy park was land-scaped by Frederick Law Olmsted to accentuate its natural glacial features and it offers an enchanting piece of countryside within the city. Locals enjoy the 1.5-mile (2.5-km) bankside path or fish in the 53-ft- (16-m-) deep glacial kettle pond (fishing requires a Massachusetts license – call 617 626 1590). The boathouse rents small sailboats, kayaks, and rowboats in summer.

3 Forest Hills Cemetery
95 Forest Hills Ave, Jamaica Plain ■ 617 524 0128

More than 100,000 graves dot the rolling landscape in this Victorian "garden cemetery," one of the first of its kind. Maps available at the entrance identify the graves of notable figures, such as poet E. E. Cummings and playwright Eugene O'Neill. Striking memorials include the bas-relief *Death Stays the Hand of the Artist* by Daniel Chester French, near the main entrance.

4 Franklin Park
Franklin Park Rd, Dorchester
■ 617 265 4084

Frederick Law Olmsted considered Franklin Park the masterpiece of his Emerald Necklace (see p19), but his vision of urban wilds has since been modified to more modern uses. The park is home to the second-oldest municipal golf course in the US and the child-friendly Franklin Park Zoo (see p53), which contrasts contemporary ecological exhibits with charming zoo architecture, such as a 1913 pagoda-style bird house.

A playground at Franklin Park Zoo

Sandy beach at tranquil Pleasure Bay

5 Pleasure Bay

South Boston's Pleasure Bay park encloses a pond-like cove of Boston Harbor with a causeway boardwalk, where locals turn out for their daily constitutionals. Castle Island, now attached to the mainland, has guarded the mouth of Boston Harbor since the first fortress was erected in 1634. As New England's oldest continually fortified site, it is now guarded by Fort Independence (c. 1851). Anglers gather on the adjacent Steel Pier and drop bait into the mass of striped bass and bluefish.

6 Centre Street

Jamaica Plain is home to many artists, musicians, and writers as well as a substantial portion of Boston's gay and lesbian community. Centre Street is the main artery and hub. There is a distinctly Latin-American flavor at the Jackson Square end, where Caribbean music shops and Cuban, Dominican, and Mexican

Centre Street

eateries abound. At the 600 block, Centre Street morphs into an urban counter-cultural village, with design boutiques, funky second-hand stores, and small cafés and restaurants.

7 Upham's Corner

Strand Theatre, 543 Columbia Rd, Dorchester ▪ 617 635 1403

The area known as Upham's Corner was founded in 1630, and its venerable Old Dorchester Burial Ground contains ethereal carved stones from this Puritan era. Today, Upham's Corner is decidedly more Caribbean than Puritan, with shops specializing in food, clothing, and the music of the islands. The Strand Theatre, a 1918 luxury movie palace and vaudeville hall, functions as an arts center and venue for live concerts and religious revival meetings.

8 Dudley Square

Hamill Gallery of Tribal Art, 2164 Washington St, Roxbury ▪ 617 442 8204 ▪ Open noon–6pm Thu–Sat Dillaway-Thomas House, 183 Roxbury St, Roxbury ▪ 617 445 3399 ▪ Call in advance for tour hours

Roxbury's Dudley Square is the heart of African-American Boston as well as the busiest hub in Boston's public transportation network. The Beaux Arts station is modeled on the great train stations of Europe. Among the square's many shops and galleries is the Hamill Gallery of Tribal Art, as much a small museum as a gallery. A few blocks from the square, the modest Georgian-style

Dillaway-Thomas House reveals Roxbury's early history, including the period when it served as HQ for the Continental Army's General John Thomas during the Siege of Boston.

⑨ Edward M. Kennedy Institute for the United States Senate

210 Morrissey Blvd, Dorchester ■ 617 740 7000 ■ 10am–5pm Tue–Sun ■ Adm ■ www.emkinstitute.org

Displaying re-creations of the US Senate Chamber and Senator Edward M. Kennedy's office, this facility provides an impressive interactive experience of how the Senate functions. With film and live actors, 'Great Senate Debates' recreates historic turning points in the Senate.

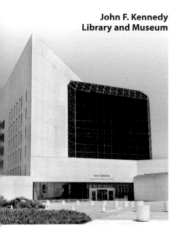

John F. Kennedy Library and Museum

⑩ John F. Kennedy Library and Museum

Columbia Point, Dorchester ■ 617 514 1600 ■ Open 9am–5pm daily ■ Adm ■ www.jfklibrary.org

This nine-story pyramidal building designed by I. M. Pei in 1977 stands like a billowing sail on Columbia Point. Inside, exhibits recount the 1,000 days of the Kennedy presidency. Kennedy was the first president to grasp the power of broadcast, and video exhibits include campaign debates, as well as coverage of his assassination and funeral.

STREET HEAT & POND COOL IN JAMAICA PLAIN

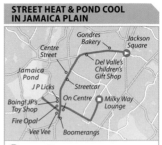

▶ AFTERNOON

The Orange Line "T" delivers you to the Latin end of Jamaica Plain's **Centre Street** at Jackson Square, where life is more Santo Domingo than "Downtown Boston". Head west and ease into the rhythm by sampling empanadas, coffee, and Latin desserts at **Gondres Bakery** *(333 Centre St)*. A walk along Centre Street serves up a cornucopia of Latino fashion and specialty shops. **Del Valle's Children's Gift Shop** *(360 Centre St)* has clothing from christening gowns and rompers to dress shoes and jewelry. Follow Centre Street as it doglegs left. Hip **Streetcar** *(488 Centre Street)* carries a large selection of boutique wines and craft beers. At **J P Licks** *(659 Centre St)* order a cone of super-premium ice cream, and continue to **Boing! JP's Toy Shop** *(667 Centre St)* to discover fun gifts for kids from one to 91. Jeweler Phil Celeste carries unique clothing, jewelry and gift items at **On Centre** *(676 Centre St)*, while **Fire Opal** *(683 Centre St)* showcases handmade American art, apparel, and jewelry. The thrift store **Boomerangs** *(716 Centre St)* has clothing and home decor. Stroll up Burroughs Street and cross Jamaicaway to **Jamaica Pond** *(see p131)* to stroll, sit in the shade, or rent a rowboat.

EVENING

Once you've worked up an appetite, return to Centre Street for dinner at **Vee Vee** *(see p135)*. Afterward, hit ultra-hip **Milky Way Lounge** *(see p134)* for a chilled beer, live music, and dancing.

See map on p130 ←

Bars and Clubs

 The Jeannie Johnston
144 South St, Jamaica Plain

This entertainment venue has plenty to offer, with an open mic on Thursdays, live local bands on Fridays, and karaoke on Saturdays, as well as a snug spot to sit with one of its 35 draft or bottled beers.

 Milky Way Lounge
284 Amory St, Jamaica Plain

Situated in JP's legendary Brewery Complex, Latinos and Jamaica Plain hipsters rub shoulders at the Milky Way. They come for the dancing, the latest local live bands, and the exceptional cosmopolitans.

 The Punk & Poet
658 East Broadway, South Boston

Stylish Irish punk pub serving good bar-friendly food (including burgers, wings and fish and chips) and a range of local and non-local beers.

4 **dbar**
1236 Dorchester Ave, Dorchester

The eclectic dinner menu disappears around 10pm, when dbar morphs into a hopping, diverse nightclub where brightly colored cocktails are a specialty. Show tunes on Tuesdays, karaoke on Fridays.

5 **Lucky's Lounge**
355 Congress St, South Boston

A Fort Point Channel underground bar that swaggers with rat-pack retro ambience, right down to the lounge acts and the unmissable Frank Sinatra tribute nights.

 The Broadway
734 East Broadway, South Boston

On weekends this watering hole is packed both inside and outside in the garden. Modern pub food hits a fairly high mark.

7 **L Street Tavern**
658A East 8th St, South Boston

One of Southie's most old-fashioned pubs, L Street serves Harpoon and Guinness on tap. The Oscar-winning movie *Good Will Hunting* was filmed here.

 Brendan Behan Pub
378 Centre St, Jamaica Plain

This Irish pub is frequented by neighborhood types with vaguely poetic pretensions, and outfitted with Guinness and Murphy's on tap. Live music most nights.

9 **Local 149**
149 P St, South Boston

This South Boston neighborhood joint features local beers on tap, creative cocktails, and some of the best New American food outside of a fancy restaurant.

10 **Doyle's Café**
3484 Washington St, Jamaica Plain

The apex of Irish-American political culture, Doyle's has been serving beer since 1882, and corned beef and cabbage on Thursdays for as long as anyone can remember.

Bar at Doyle's Café

Restaurants

PRICE CATEGORIES

For a three-course meal for one with half a bottle of wine (or equivalent meal), taxes, and extra charges.

$ under $40 $$ $40–$60 $$$ over $60

1 Coppersmith
40 W 3rd St, South Boston
■ 617 658 3452 ■ $$

This vast converted warehouse has an American bistro restaurant as well as a casual café serving global fare. Try the BBQ popcorn, which is excellent.

Bright decor at Tres Gatos

2 Tres Gatos
470 Centre St, Jamaica Plain
■ 617 477 4851 ■ $

This combination tapas bar and book/music store features authentic Spanish bar dishes along with some inventive variants.

3 Yellowdoor Taqueria
2297 Dorchester Ave ■ 857 267 4201 ■ Closed L ■ $

This snazzy Mexican bar in Lower Mills specializes in craft cocktails, rare tequila, and local beer. Food includes innovative tacos, healthy salads, and great ceviches.

4 Ashmont Grill
MAP D4 ■ 555 Talbot Ave, Dorchester ■ 617 825 4300 ■ Open daily for D and L Fri, brunch Sat & Sun ■ $$

Veteran chef Chris Douglass uses local produce to conjure up contemporary bistro delights.

5 El Miami Restaurant
381 Centre St, Jamaica Plain
■ 617 522 4644 ■ $

This place is the self-proclaimed "King of the Cuban sandwiches." Check out the photos of the Latino pro baseball players who often eat here when in town.

6 Tavolo
1918 Dorchester Ave, Dorchester ■ 617 822 1918
■ Closed L ■ $$

Superb, rustic Italian cuisine emphasizes fresh market dining in this Ashmont neighborhood.

7 Ten Tables
597 Centre St, Jamaica Plain
■ 617 524 8810 ■ Closed L ■ $$$

This small venue has just ten tables with, an equally compact but rewarding menu, such as scallops on minted pea tendrils.

8 Vee Vee
763 Centre St, Jamaica Plain
■ 617 522 0145 ■ Closed L and Mon
■ $$

Delectable American bistro fare makes this restaurant a favorite with local foodies, especially since many dishes have vegetarian versions. The Sunday brunch is very popular.

9 Bella Luna
280 Armory St, Jamaica Plain
■ 617 524 6060 ■ $$

The dining room adjacent to the Milky Way Lounge, Bella Luna shoots the moon with bright salads, rib-sticking Italian fare such as chicken marsala, and their signature gourmet pizzas.

10 Blue Nile
389 Centre St, Jamaica Plain
■ 617 522 6453 ■ Closed Mon ■ $

Ethiopian home-style food celebrates fresh vegetables as well as meats and fish, and there's plenty of choice for vegans as well. *Teff injera*, the sourdough pancakes that double as utensils, are made on the premises.

See map on p130

Boston Streetsmart

Boston street signs

Getting To and Around Boston **138**

Practical Information **140**

Places to Stay **146**

General Index **152**

Acknowledgments **158**

Getting To and Around Boston

Arriving by Air

Logan International Airport (BOS) is located 2 miles (3 km) northeast of Downtown. Over 50 international and domestic airlines serve the area.

Transportation to central Boston is accessed from the baggage claim area. Taxis wait at all terminals but airport fees can make a downtown trip expensive ($25–$35). Logan Airport is also served by private taxi companies, such as **Star Shuttle**, as well as ride sharing companies. The MBTA Silver Line bus to South Station is free here and takes 15 to 30 minutes. Free buses link terminals to the Blue Line subway. Shuttle services are available via **Massport** to Downtown Boston and to locations throughout Massachusetts.

For the scenic water route, take the Route 66 airport shuttle to Logan Dock. **Boston Water Taxi** serves Logan and the waterfront. **Rowes Wharf Water Transport** provides direct service to and from Rowes Wharf.

Several international and some domestic charters use **Manchester Airport** (MHT) in New Hampshire, 50 miles (79 km) from Boston, and **TF Green Airport** (PVD), near Providence, Rhode Island, 59 miles (95 km) from Boston. Buses to Boston run from both.

Arriving by Train

The **Amtrak** intercity rail transportation arrives into Boston at South Station

(Atlantic and Summer streets). Frequent New York trains take 3 to 5 hours. Several daily trains arrive from Brunswick and Portland, Maine.

Arriving by Car

Most major northeast highways converge on Boston, with I-95 (also known as Route 128) bypassing the city center. I-90, the Massachusetts Turnpike, comes in from the west. I-93 crosses the city north to south as an underground expressway, known as the Thomas P. "Tip" O'Neill Jr. Tunnel. Watch signs carefully for exits. The Zakim bridge, connecting underground and surface highways, provides a northern gateway to Boston.

Arriving by Bus

The city's primary bus station, **South Station Transportation Center**, is used by a dozen companies providing intercity service, as well as Amtrak and the MBTA subway system. **Greyhound** connects with over 3,700 locations, and offers lowcost passes. Other lines include **Megabus**, **Bolt Bus**, and **Peter Pan**.

Arriving by Ship

Cruise ships dock at Black Falcon Terminal, South Boston, which is a $20 taxi ride away from Downtown. On Port of Call days, the local trolley tour companies (see p143) offer services to popular city destinations.

Traveling by Public Transportation

Boston's subway and trolley system (the "T"), buses, commuter rail, and ferries are run by **MBTA** (Massachusetts Bay Transportation Authority). The subway and trolley system gets you close to most places in the city. Fares are $2.75 to almost everywhere, and buying a reuseable, rechargeable CharlieCard reduces the fare to $2.25.

The MBTA bus system enlarges the transit network to cover more than 1,000 miles (1,620 km). Buses run less frequently than the "T." The Silver Line, technically a "T" line, runs buses, providing quick trips to airport or cruise ship terminals. Make sure you have exact change or a CharlieCard for the bus. Maps are available on the MBTA website or at the office at Downtown Crossing.

A pass gives you unlimited MBTA travel, including inner harbor ferries, and can be bought on a CharlieCard for $12 (one day) and $21.25 (seven days) at most subway stations.

Traveling by Car

The least efficient way to get around Downtown is driving, which can be stressful. Locals drive quite aggressively, and the narrow streets are laid out in a confusing manner with little signage. There are few gas stations, limited parking with time-of-day restrictions, one-way streets, and traffic circles. For drivers unfamiliar with the city, an up-to-date GPS and advance planning are essential.

Parking lots are very expensive, costing about $35 per day or about $12 for one hour in the Boston Common Garage in the city center. Other parking lots in the area charge more. On-street parking meters have a two-hour limit, residents-only rules are strictly enforced, and fines are high.

Car rental companies have desks at Logan Airport. Drivers must be between 21 and 75 years with a valid license. All agencies require a credit card or cash deposit.

Collision damage waiver and liability insurances are highly recommended.

Traveling by Taxi

Taxis can be hired on the street in the Downtown area or at taxi stands. You can also call **Metro Cab**, **Boston Cab Association**, **ITOA**, or **Cambridge Cab Company** to arrange a pick up. **Uber** and **Lyft** let you summon a ride share car by smartphone, billing your credit card.

Traveling by Water Taxi and Ferry

Boston Harbor Cruises offers ferries to Salem and Provincetown from

Long Wharf. The **Bay State Cruise Company** connects the World Trade Center with Provincetown, and the inexpensive **MBTA Harbor Express** connects Long Wharf to Charlestown Navy Yard.

Walking and Cycling

Downtown Boston is compact and easy to get around on foot. It has many bike paths including on some major streets. Cycling on highways is illegal and riding on sidewalks is discouraged or illegal. **Hubway** has bike sharing at 200 stations throughout the city.

DIRECTORY

ARRIVING BY AIR

Boston Water Taxi
☏ 617 227 4320
w bostonharborcruises.com

Logan International Airport
☏ 617 561 1800
w massport.com

Manchester Airport
☏ 603 624 6556
w flymanchester.com

Massport
w massport.com

TF Green Airport
☏ 401 691 2471
w pvdairport.com

Rowes Wharf Water Transport
☏ 617 406 8584
w roweswharfwater transport.com

Star Shuttle
☏ 617 230 6005
w starshuttleboston.com

ARRIVING BY TRAIN

Amtrak
☏ 800 872 7245
w amtrak.com

ARRIVING BY BUS

BoltBus
☏ 877 265 8287
w boltbus.com

Greyhound
☏ 800 231 2222
w greyhound.com

Megabus
☏ 877 462 6342
w megabus.com

Peter Pan
☏ 401 751 8800
w peterpanbus.com

South Station Transportation Center
700 Atlantic Ave
w south-station.net

TRAVELING BY PUBLIC TRANSPORTATION

MBTA
☏ 617 222 3200
w mbta.com

TRAVELING BY TAXI

Boston Cab Association
☏ 617 536 5010
w bostoncab.us

Cambridge Cab Company
☏ 617 547 3000
w cambridgecabco.com

ITOA
☏ 617 268 1313
w itoataxi.com

Lyft
w www.lyft.com

Metro Cab
☏ 617 782 5500
w boston-cab.com

Uber
w uber.com

TRAVELING BY WATER TAXI AND FERRY

Bay State Cruise Company
☏ 617 748 1428
w baystatecruise company.com

Boston Harbor Cruises
☏ 617 227 4320
w bostonharborcruises.com

MBTA Harbor Express
☏ 617 222 6999
w mbta.com

WALKING AND CYCLING

Hubway
w thehubway.com

Practical Information

Passports and Visas

Canadian and Mexican visitors require valid passports to enter the US. Citizens of 38 countries, including most European nations, Australia, and New Zealand, do not need a visa, but must have a passport and apply to enter in advance via the **Electronic System for Travel Authorization (ESTA)**. All other visitors require a tourist visa and passport to enter, and will be photographed and have fingerprints checked by the **Transportation Security Administration**. Regulations may change, so check well in advance of travel with the US Department of State for the latest information.

A number of countries, including the **UK**, **Canada**, and **Ireland**, have consulates here and can provide limited consular assistance to their nationals.

Customs and Immigration

Nonresident travelers to the US need to complete a **Customs and Border Protection Agency** form. Passengers may carry $100 in gifts; one liter of alcohol as beer, wine, or liquor (age 21 years or older); and one carton of cigarettes, 50 cigars (not Cuban), or two kg (4.4 lbs) smoking tobacco without incurring tax.

Travel Safety Advice

Visitors can get up-to-date travel safety information from the **UK Foreign and Commonwealth Office**, the **US Department of State**, and the **Australian Department of Foreign Affairs and Trade**.

Travel Insurance

Medical insurance is highly recommended for international travelers, as costs for health and dental care can be very high. Insurance against trip cancellation, air travel delays, and lost baggage is advisable. Car rental agencies offer vehicle and liability insurance, but always check your policy.

Health

No vaccinations will be required for visiting the US. Pack medications in their original, labeled containers. You can carry unused syringes and injectable prescription medication. Your hotel will usually recommend a doctor if you need one.

Hospitals such as the **Massachusetts General Hospital**, **Boston Medical Center**, **Tufts Medical Center**, **Partners Urgent Care**, and Beth Israel Deaconess Medical Center offer emergency and urgent walk-in care. Minor injury clinics such as those run by **CVS** are available through the city. Central Boston has a **CVS 24-hour Pharmacy**. Some pharmacies also have nurse practitioners.

Personal Security

Boston is usually safe in the tourist areas. However, always be alert to your surroundings, leave your valuables and passport in a hotel safe, get a receipt for stored luggage, and be discreet with expensive jewelry, cameras, and phones. Split cash and cards between wallets and pockets, keep wallets in inside pockets, and carry a cross-body purse. Keep copies of your documents and ID separately.

If you will be out late, ask your hotel concierge for advice related to your specific destination. The likelihood of stolen property being recovered is slim, but you should file a claim with the **Boston Police Department** and keep a copy for the insurance company. Within the MBTA's service area, you can also ask the **MBTA Transit Police** for help. Note the taxi company, bus line, or metro route you use to help retrieve lost belongings. If you misplace your passport, contact your embassy. Call your credit card company or bank at once to report lost or stolen cards or traveler's checks.

Emergency Services

For **ambulance, medical, police, and fire brigade** services, call the national emergency number 911 and give your location and details about the problem.

Travelers with Specific Needs

All facilities renovated or newly built since 1987 are legally required to provide wheelchair-accessible entrances and restrooms.

Government buildings, museums, and theaters are accessible, but call ahead to verify that tours can meet your needs. It is best to call historic buildings, hotels, and restaurants in advance to ask about amenities. The website of the **Greater Boston Convention & Visitors Bureau** has access information and contact numbers for a range of places and tours.

All establishments allow guide dogs, and most busy road intersections have audio signals for safe crossing times.

Most **MBTA** commuter rail lines, buses, subways, and ferries accommodate wheelchairs. Check its website for details. The **Boston Cab Association** (see p139) will send an accessible vehicle on request. **Logan International Airport** (see p139) has accessible restrooms, elevators, and ramps plus a list of accessible transportation to and from the airport on its website.

Fenway Park (see p117) has accessible elevators, spaces for wheelchair users, and seats for the hearing or visually impaired. Listening devices are available.

Currency and Banking

The US currency is the dollar ($), made up of 100 cents. The most common denominations of bills are $1, $5, $10, and $20, with larger denominations also available. Cents come in 1 (penny), 5 (nickel), 10 (dime), and 25 (quarter) cent coins. Convert some currency at the airport for immediate expenses, then change larger amounts at a bank or ATM later for a better rate. Currency bureaus such as **Travelex** can be found at Logan Airport and other sites.

A major credit card will be needed for car rentals, hotels, and restaurants. Most services will accept Visa, Mastercard, and American Express. You will need cash for street vendors and buses.

DIRECTORY

PASSPORTS AND VISAS
Canada
MAP M6 ■ 3 Copley Place, Suite 400
⚑ boston.gc.ca

Electronic System for Travel Authorization (ESTA)
⚑ esta.cbp.dhs.gov/esta

Ireland
MAP M5 ■ 535 Boylston St, 5th Floor
⚑ dfa.ie/irish-consulate/boston

Transportation Security Administration
⚑ tsa.gov/travel

UK
MAP E3 ■ One Broadway, Cambridge
⚑ ukinusa.fco.gov.uk

CUSTOMS AND IMMIGRATION
Customs and Border Protection Agency
Visa Waiver Program, customs information
⚑ cbp.gov/travel

TRAVEL SAFETY ADVICE
Australian Department of Foreign Affairs and Trade
⚑ dfat.gov.au
⚑ smartraveller.gov.au

UK Foreign and Commonwealth Office
⚑ gov.uk/foreign-travel-advice

US Department of State
⚑ state.gov/travel

HEALTH
Beth Israel Deaconess Medical Center
⚑ bidmc.org

Boston Medical Center
⚑ bmc.org

CVS
36 White St, Cambridge
☎ 617 876 5519

CVS 24-Hour Pharmacy
MAP L5 ■ 587 Boylston St
☎ 617 437 8414

Massachusetts General Hospital
⚑ massgeneral.org

Partners Urgent Care
⚑ partnersurgentcare.org

Tufts Medical Center
⚑ tuftsmedicalcenter.org

PERSONAL SECURITY
Boston Police Department
☎ 617 343 4500

MBTA Transit Police
☎ 617 222 1212

EMERGENCY SERVICES
Ambulance, Medical, Police, and Fire Brigade
☎ 911

TRAVELERS WITH SPECIFIC NEEDS
Greater Boston Convention & Visitors Bureau
⚑ bostonusa.com/plan-your-trip/getting-around/accessiblity

MBTA
⚑ mbta.com/accessibility

CURRENCY AND BANKING
Travelex
⚑ travelex.com

Telephone and Internet

US phone numbers are ten digits long. The first three digits are the area code, which is 617 or 857 for Boston, Cambridge, Brookline, and Somerville. The area codes for the region around Boston are 339, 351, 508, 774, 781 and 978. Dial 0 for the operator, and 411 for directory assistance (fee). To make an overseas call, dial 011, country code, city code, and number; to go via an operator, dial 01 instead of 011.

Public telephones are rare and making calls from your hotel room can be expensive. If you plan to use a cell phone, check with your provider about service in the US before traveling. **Cellular Abroad**, **Cellhire**, and others rent phones for calls, or you can buy a disposable phone at many outlets.

Most hotels offer free Wi-Fi, but some may levy a charge. Many public places have free Wi-Fi.

Postal Services

Many hotels sell stamps and will mail your letters. Flat rate envelopes and boxes for all destinations are available at **US Postal Service** post offices.

Newspapers and Magazines

The daily newspapers are the **Boston Globe** and **Boston Herald**. The free weekly **DigBoston** has arts and entertainment listings, and the monthly **Boston Magazine** (see p144) has comprehensive restaurant reviews.

Opening Hours

Office hours are 9am to 5pm. Stores open at 10am or 11am and close at 6pm or 7pm Monday to Saturday. Some remain open later, generally on Thursday evening and during the tourist season, while on Sunday hours are usually noon to 6pm. Malls open Monday to Saturday from 9am or 10am to 8pm or 9pm, and noon to 6pm Sunday. Grocery stores generally open 8am to 9pm daily, or longer. Pharmacy hours vary, from 8am to 6pm or later. Some are open 24 hours.

Most banks are open 9am to 4pm or 5pm Monday to Friday, and some also open on Saturday morning. Museums are usually open 10am (noon on Sun) to 5pm, but check before making your plans.

MBTA trains begin at about 5am Monday to Saturday, 6am on Sunday, and end between midnight and 1am every night. Each line and each station varies so check ahead.

Time Difference

Boston is on Eastern Standard Time (EST), three hours ahead of California and five hours behind the UK. Daylight Saving Time starts at 2am on the second Sunday in March and ends on the first Sunday in November.

Electrical Appliances

The standard US electric current is 110 volts and 60 Hz current. An adapter will be required for all European appliances.

Driving

Visitors with valid licenses from most countries can drive here, but it is best to bring an International Driving Permit, especially if the license is not from a qualifying country, is not in English, or does not have a photograph.

Weather

Summers can be humid and hot (over 81° F/27° C), but pack a variety of clothing as the weather can be changeable, with rainy, cold, or windy days. Winters can be very cold (21° F/-6° C in January) with snow, ice, and wind, and the weather may change through the day. Spring and fall weather is generally pleasant, with warm days and cooler mornings and evenings.

Visitor Information

The **Greater Boston Convention & Visitors Bureau** has information on hotels, shops, dining, sights, and transportation on their site. You can also call them or stop by the Boston Common Visitor Center or the information booth at the Prudential Center. The **Boston National Historical Park** visitor center at Faneuil Hall also has plenty of visitor information.

The **Cambridge Office of Tourism** has an interactive website and phone support, or you can drop by the main office or the information booth in Harvard Square. The **City of Boston** site and the **Massachusetts Office of Travel & Tourism** are also useful resources.

Trips and Tours

Several trolley tours start at the Boston Common Visitor Center, including **Old Town Trolley Tours** and **Upper Deck Trolley Tours**, which offer narrated sightseeing on old-fashioned trolley buses, as well as seasonal and themed tours. The tours permit re-boarding all day, making them easy transits to major sites.

Boston Harbor Cruises offers harbor and whale-watching tours, as well as a ferry service to the Boston Harbor Islands, Salem, and Provincetown. Sightseeing and sunset tours of the Charles River on small cruise boats are offered by the **Charles Riverboat Company**.

Boston Duck Tours, especially popular with families, use open-topped amphibious vehicles that both trundle through the streets and plunge into the Charles River.

Enthusiastic volunteers from **Boston By Foot** share their love of the city on a range of guided walks. Knowledgeable rangers from Boston National Historical Park also run tours of the Freedom Trail (see pp12–13), the Black Heritage Trail (see 82), and the Charlestown Navy Yard (see pp36–7). **Frederick Law Olmsted National Historic Site** rangers run tours of portions of the Emerald Necklace (see p19), as well as tours of the office and grounds by reservation.

The **New England Aquarium** (see pp38–9) runs whale-watching trips with trained marine biologists. Ships with around 200–400 passengers head out to the Stellwagen Bank whale feeding grounds from March to mid-November.

Visitors can sample the colorful flavors of Boston's ethnic neigh-borhoods on foodie tours. **Boston Food Tours** offers tastings, tips, and insights on the lively Italian food markets, restaurants, and cuisine of the North End. **Free Tours by Foot** explores Chinatown's cuisine.

Urban Adventours runs narrated bicycle tours that include an overview of Boston highlights plus a few places off the tourist trail. You can enjoy a ride along the Charles River, a sunset spin along the city's waterfront, or a fall foliage tour through the Emerald Necklace.

Movie buffs will enjoy a walk to iconic Boston film and television locations with **On Location Tours**.

DIRECTORY

TELEPHONE AND INTERNET

Cellhire
w cellhire.com

Cellular Abroad
w cellularabroad.com

POSTAL SERVICES

US Postal Service
w usps.com

NEWSPAPERS AND MAGAZINES

Boston Globe
w bostonglobe.com

Boston Herald
w bostonherald.com

DigBoston
w digboston.com

VISITOR INFORMATION

Boston National Historical Park
w nps.gov/bost

Cambridge Office of Tourism
(617 441 2884
w cambridgeusa.org

City of Boston
w cityofboston.gov

Greater Boston Convention & Visitors Bureau
(617 536 4100
w bostonusa.com

Massachusetts Office of Travel & Tourism
(617 973 8500
w mass-vacation.com

TRIPS AND TOURS

Boston By Foot
w bostonbyfoot.org

Boston Duck Tours
w bostonducktours.com

Boston Food Tours
w bostonfoodtours.com

Boston Harbor Cruises
w bostonharbor cruises.com

Charles Riverboat Company
w charlesriverboat.com

Frederick Law Olmsted National Historic Site
w nps.gov/frla

Free Tours by Foot
w freetoursbyfoot.com

Old Town Trolley Tours
w trolleytours.com/boston

On Location Tours
w onlocationtours.com/boston-tours/

Upper Deck Trolley Tours
w bostonsupertours.com/upper-deck-trolley-tours

Urban Adventours
w urbanadventours.com

Shopping

Shopping is an extremely popular activity in Boston, and most of the city's best shopping areas can be found featured in this guide. A fantastic variety of merchandise in every price range is available; most stores accept major credit cards; and there is no state sales tax on clothing, except for items of clothing retailing in excess of $175, when a 6.25 percent tax is charged on the amount over $175.

Back Bay offers two luxury shopping plazas: **Copley Place** (see p68) with 75 distinctive stores, including Neiman Marcus, Jimmy Choo, and Louis Vuitton; and the shops at **Prudential Center** (see p88), featuring Saks Fifth Avenue and 70 more stores. Nearby **Newbury Street** (see pp24–5) is where the big-name fashion designers have shops, as well as high-end home furnishings, antiques, and art galleries. The stores on Newbury Street get funkier toward Massachusetts Avenue. One block away, Boylston Street has plenty of top sporting goods emporiums and famous-name chain stores.

Historic Beacon Hill is home to a cluster of exceptional antique shops along **Charles Street** (see p69) that are surrounded by exclusive little clothing and shoe boutiques. In studenty Cambridge, **Harvard Square** (see p69) is well known for its fine selection of bookstores, along with about 70 shops and chain stores concentrated in a small area.

The lively carnival-like atmosphere of historic **Faneuil Hall and Quincy Market** (see p101) creates a fun shopping experience, with buskers, chain stores, and an eclectic collection of pushcart stalls offering souvenirs, handmade jewelry, local crafts, and clothing.

Truly unique gifts and souvenirs can be found in Boston's museum shops and gift stores at major attractions. Most of these shops carry high-quality specialty items related to their collections, as well as popular lower-cost souvenirs. The gift shops at the **Museum of Fine Arts** (see pp28–31), the **Museum of Science** (see pp16–17), and the **Isabella Stewart Gardner Museum** (see pp34–5) particularly merit a visit. Also make sure you check out the specialty museums, such as the **USS Constitution Museum** (see p36) and the **New England Aquarium** (see pp38–9).

There are several large shopping malls located just outside the city. West of the city, **The Shops at Chestnut Hill** mall has Bloomingdales and 60 high-quality shops and boutiques. The huge **Burlington Mall**, north of the city, has Nordstrom, Macy's, and almost 200 other popular stores. **Natick Mall** is one of the largest in New England with 200-plus stores, and is anchored by Neiman Marcus, Nordstrom, and Macy's. There are two outlet malls, **Wrentham Village Premium Outlets** with 170 high-end brands, and the smaller **Assembly Row** in Somerville, complete with dining, LEGOLAND Discovery Center, a hotel, and a waterfront park.

Dining

Boston restaurants span a diverse scene, ranging from expensive celebrity chef establishments downtown and in Back Bay to the affordable eateries found near the universities. Great meals can be eaten in the city's many small, independent, and often ethnic eateries: Italian in the North End, Asian in Chinatown and the Theater District, and creative contemporary dishes in the South End. And when the weather is warm, choose a sidewalk café along Newbury, or head to the waterfront for clam chowder, oyster bars, and ocean-fresh seafood.

Boston being a major fishing port, fresh seafood is plentiful. City favorites are the sweet-tasting, large-clawed American lobster, young haddock or cod, known locally as scrod, and bluefish, which makes a stronger-flavored meal. You'll need to know your seafood terminology, too – a quahog is a large clam, while prized local oysters are known as American bluepoints.

Check out the latest restaurant reviews in **Boston Magazine** and make a reservation online with **Open Table**. Note that the most popular restaurants need to be booked at least a month in advance. You could also check for cancellations by calling the restaurant the same day. Some places seat guests as they arrive, so it's best to reach by 6pm.

Breakfast is generally served from 7am to 10am, lunch between 11:30am and 2pm, and dinner from 5:30pm to 10pm.

A seven percent tax is added to the final bill in Boston and Cambridge, and a tip of 15–20 percent of the total amount is expected. Alcoholic drinks are available in many restaurants. The legal age for drinking alcohol is 21 years, and a photo ID may be requested from patrons of all ages.

Accommodation

Boston hotels tend to be expensive, especially those in central Boston, close to principal tourist attractions – namely Back Bay, Downtown, Beacon Hill, and the Financial District. Hotels and inns outside the city center are a better bargain. Travelers accustomed to large motel rooms may be surprised by the small dimensions of some rooms in older Boston hotels, especially those in the lower price range. European-style twin-bedded rooms are fairly rare; most rooms have two double beds or one king- or queen-size bed.

Rates vary with the season, and also on how full the property will be on a particular date. Rates are highest between May and October, and when special events are in progress. The **Greater Boston Convention & Visitors Bureau** *(see p143)* offers a comprehensive list of hotels, but does not provide a reservation service. For the best rates, check online on **Kayak** or **Expedia** and then call the

hotel to ask for their best rate and any special packages they may offer. Hotel tax in the Boston area is 14.45 percent, and room rates are usually quoted without tax.

There are other options for lodging beyond hotels, and if you are willing to forego the amenities and services of large hotels, many of these options offer lower prices.

For bed-and-breakfast properties, many of which are in historic or characterful homes and include a full breakfast and often Wi-Fi as well, contact the **Bed and Breakfast Agency of Boston**.

Savings can be made in "efficiency" (self-catering) apartments or rooms. Furnished apartments and homes often provide more space and amenities at a lower price. They generally provide a full kitchen but no housekeeping service and are often located in residential areas. They can usually be booked through the same agencies as bed-and-breakfast places, or via **Vacation Rentals** and **Vacation Rentals by Owner**, agencies with many self-catering properties on their books.

Another budget option is **Airbnb**, which lists both furnished apartments and shared-living-space bedrooms within a private residence. Boston also has several hostels listed on **Hostels.com**, often with a choice of en-suite or dorm accommodations, including the smart and central **Hostelling International**. You can even stay overnight on a tall ship moored in Boston Harbor with **Liberty Fleet**.

DIRECTORY

SHOPPING

Assembly Row
617 440 5565
assemblyrow.com

Burlington Mall
781 272 8668
simon.com/mall/
burlington-mall

Natick Mall
natickmall.com

**The Shops at
Chestnut Hill**
617 965 3038
simon.com/
mall/the-shops-at-
chestnut-hill

**Wrentham Village
Premium Outlets**
508 384 2876
premiumoutlets.com/
outlet/wrentham-village

DINING

Boston Magazine
bostonmagazine.com

Open Table
opentable.com

ACCOMMODATION

Airbnb
airbnb.com

**Bed and Breakfast
Agency of Boston**
47 Commercial Wharf
617 720 3540
boston-bnbagency.
com

Expedia
expedia.com

Hostelling International
19 Stuart Street
bostonhostel.org

Hostels.com
hostels.com

Kayak
kayak.com

Liberty Fleet
67 Long Wharf
617 742 0333
libertyfleet.com

Vacation Rentals
vacationrentals.com

**Vacation Rentals
by Owner**
vrbo.com

Places to Stay

PRICE CATEGORIES

For a standard, double room per night (with breakfast if included), taxes and extra charges.

$ under $250 **$$** $250 to $450 **$$$** over $450

Luxury Hotels

Eliot Hotel

MAP J5 = 370 Commonwealth Ave, 02215 = 617 267 1607 = www.eliothotel.com = $$

Back Bay grace and charm characterize this late 19th-century landmark hotel. Visiting musicians and baseball teams alike enjoy the spacious suites. Uni (see p93), the ground-floor restaurant, is one of Boston's most acclaimed and provides room service for the Eliot's guests.

Langham, Boston

MAP Q3 = 250 Franklin St, 02110 = 617 451 1900 = www.langhamhotels. com = $$

The extremely posh Langham occupies a jewel of an Art Nouveau building, the former Federal Reserve bank in the heart of the Financial District. Spacious rooms feature modernized Second Empire decor with rich brocades.

Liberty Hotel

MAP F3 = 215 Charles St, 02114 = 617 224 4000 = www.libertyhotel.com = $$

Dramatic design has transformed the historic Charles Street Jail into an elegant boutique hotel with a soaring lobby. Basketball and hockey teams stay here, as TD Garden is nearby.

Revere Hotel

MAP N5 = 200 Stuart Street, 02116 = 617 428 1800 = www.reverehotel. com = $$

This sleek, hip hotel is two blocks from Boston Common and close to the Theater District. Every elegant room has its own private balcony. The rooftop pool and bar serves lunch in summer. The Emerald Lounge is a local favorite.

The Millennium Bostonian

MAP Q2 = Faneuil Hall Marketplace, 02109 = 617 523 3600 = www. millenniumhotels.com = $$

Rooms run the gamut from tiny to palatial in this elegant and swanky oasis close to bustling Faneuil Hall and Quincy Market (see p101), but all feature lovely city views. There is also an excellent on-site fitness center.

Boston Harbor Hotel

MAP R3 = 70 Rowes Wharf, 02110 = 617 439 7000 = www.bhh.com = $$$

To enjoy one of the most beautiful locations in the city to the full, request a room with a harbor view and private balcony. There's no need to go anywhere else as you will find restaurants, a fitness center, and spa all on site.

Four Seasons

MAP N4 = 200 Boylston St, 02116 = 617 338 4400 = www.fourseasons.com = $$$

Rock stars and visiting dignitaries often select the low-key luxury of this hotel on the edge of the Theater District. The lobby-level Bristol Lounge is a favorite spot for striking business deals, and the indoor pool is an added bonus.

Mandarin Oriental

MAP K6 = 776 Boylston St, 02199 = 617 535 8888 = www.mandarinoriental. com = $$$

Situated in the heart of Back Bay, the Mandarin Oriental has some of the city's largest luxury rooms, which are furnished with designer linens, huge bathtubs, and state-of-the-art electronics. Many guests stay on site just to enjoy the full-service spa.

Ritz-Carlton, Boston Common

MAP N4 = 10 Avery St, 02111 = 617 574 7100 = www.ritzcarlton.com = $$$

This classy hotel is on the upper levels of the tallest building overlooking the Common. The elegant rooms offer a wealth of high-tech and luxury amenities. Guests can use the fitness center for a nominal charge.

Taj Boston

MAP M4 = 15 Arlington St, 02116 = 617 536 5700 = www.tajhotels.com = $$$

The 1927 "original" Boston Ritz benefits from a great location on the edge of the Common and had a thorough restoration in 2002 to revive its old-fashioned glory. This grande dame epitomizes opulence, decorum, and "old Boston" style. The lobby bar is legendary.

XV Beacon

MAP P3 ▪ 15 Beacon St, 02108 ▪ 617 670 1500 ▪ www.xvbeacon.com ▪ $$$

The design-conscious decor and extraordinary attention to detail makes this chic but cozy boutique hotel in Beacon Hill a favorite with business executives. With just 63 rooms, all with high-tech extras, it is one of the most masculine of the city's modern hotels.

Deluxe Hotels

Ames Hotel

MAP G3 ▪ 1 Court St, 02108 ▪ 617 979 8100 ▪ www.ameshotel.com ▪ $$

An elegant contemporary hotel, housed in a land-mark building in the heart of Downtown Boston, the Ames often has excellent weekend rates because it is mainly a business hotel. Suites retain their original fireplaces along-side the windows with dramatic Romanesque arches. The contrasting minimalist room design tends toward the soothing rather than the stark.

Battery Wharf Hotel

MAP H2 ▪ 3 Battery Wharf, 02109 ▪ 617 657 1834 ▪ www.battery wharfhotelboston.com ▪ $$

Situated at the edge of the North End, this luxu-rious hotel commands the mouth of Boston Harbor. Guests benefit from a well-equipped fitness center and a luxury spa.

The Charles Hotel

MAP B2 ▪ 1 Bennett St, Cambridge, 02138 ▪ 617 864 1200 ▪ www.charles hotel.com ▪ $$

Extra touches, such as handmade quilts hanging on the walls, personalize the comfortable rooms at this modern hotel on the edge of Harvard Square. There's an indoor pool, an outstanding jazz club – the Regattabar (see p128) – and Henrietta's Table, serving regional foods.

The Colonnade

MAP K6 ▪ 120 Huntington Ave, 02116 ▪ 617 424 7000 ▪ www. colonnadehotel.com ▪ $$

Often used by upscale tour groups, the Colonnade has some of the largest and most comfortable rooms in Back Bay, as well as the city's only outdoor rooftop pool.

Hotel Marlowe

MAP F2 ▪ 25 Edwin H. Land Blvd, Cambridge, 02141 ▪ 617 868 8000 ▪ www.hotelmarlowe. com ▪ $$

Located behind the Museum of Science, this sleek hotel creates a self-contained world of com-fort with internet access, evening wine receptions, and a fitness center.

Nine Zero

MAP G3–G4 ▪ 90 Tremont St, 02108 ▪ 617 722 5800 ▪ www.ninezerohotel. com ▪ $$

Marrying sleek steel, chrome, and glass with warm wood and designer furniture, Nine Zero achieves a contemporary look with a soft edge. Its location on the Downtown Crossing corner of Boston Common is convenient.

Residence Inn Boston Back Bay / Fenway

MAP D5 ▪ 125 Brookline Ave, 02215 ▪ 617 236 8787 ▪ www.residence innbackbay.com ▪ $$

The Residence Inn is an upscale, contempo-rary extended-stay hotel that overlooks Fenway Park. Its suites offer separate living and dining areas and a full kitchen, plus amenities that include luxury bedding and free Wi-Fi. Guests can also take advantage of the com-plimentary breakfast and lounge. It's within walking distance of restaurants and shops.

Royal Sonesta

MAP F2 ▪ 5 Cambridge Pkwy, Cambridge, 02142 ▪ 617 806 4200 ▪ www. sonesta.com ▪ $$

An excellent restaurant, outstanding art collection, and striking riverside location make Royal Sonesta a top choice for aesthetes. Bargain summer family pack-ages often available.

Seaport Hotel

1 Seaport Lane, 02210 ▪ 617 385 4000 ▪ www. seaportboston.com ▪ $$

Connected by a walkway to the World Trade Center, the Seaport was one of the first to pioneer the South Boston Waterfront. Rooms are large and comfortable, and the pool is a bonus, as are regular shuttles to Downtown.

The Verb Hotel
MAP D5 ▪ 1271 Boylston St, 02215 ▪ 617 566 4500 ▪ www.theverbhotel.com ▪ $$

In the shadow of Fenway Park, this trendy, retro-themed hotel is in demand whenever there's a big event around the corner. The stylish atmosphere attracts younger crowds looking to celebrate.

Marriott Long Wharf
MAP R2 ▪ 296 State St, 02109 ▪ 617 227 0800 ▪ www.marriottlong wharf.com ▪ $$$

The waterfront location means most of the bright, spacious rooms have superb harbor or city views. Waterline, the casual bar-restaurant, is perfect for a cocktail.

Hip/Historic Stays

Beacon Hill Hotel & Bistro
MAP N3 ▪ 25 Charles St, 02114 ▪ 617 723 7575 ▪ www.beaconhillhotel. com ▪ $$

This townhouse hotel is located mere steps from Boston Common. Beacon Hill's rooms are mostly small but very Euro-chic, and there's a bistro that serves guests breakfast (included in the rates). There's also a roof deck.

Boston Park Plaza
MAP M5 ▪ 64 Arlington St, 02116 ▪ 617 426 2000 ▪ www.bostonpark plaza.com ▪ $$

The Park Plaza, built in 1927, is Boston's largest historic hotel. Sensitive restoration has thankfully reinstated some of its old glamour. Popular with convention-goers, tour packagers, and business travelers, it is convenient for Back Bay and the Theater District.

The Boxer Boston
MAP P2 ▪ 107 Merrimac St, 02114 ▪ 617 624 0202 ▪ www.theboxerboston. com ▪ $$

This stylish boutique hotel offers rooms and suites that show off a sleek "industrial-chic" design and are equipped with all the latest amenities. The Boxer is centrally located between North End and Beacon Hill, making it ideal for exploring the city on foot.

Fairmont Copley Plaza
MAP L5 ▪ 138 St James Ave, 02116 ▪ 617 267 5300 ▪ www.fairmont.com ▪ $$

This sister hotel of New York's Plaza has been a Copley Square landmark since 1912. The public areas of the Fairmont are opulent, its rooms are small but very comfortable, and its suites are truly grand.

Gryphon House
MAP D5 ▪ 9 Bay State Rd, 02215 ▪ 617 375 9003 ▪ www.innboston.com ▪ $$

This 1895 brownstone townhouse boasts huge, elegant rooms with fireplaces, wet bars, and high-speed internet. A quiet spot, convenient for Back Bay or the Fenway.

Hotel InterContinental
MAP H4 ▪ 510 Atlantic Ave, 02110 ▪ 617 217 5030 ▪ www.interconti nentalboston.com ▪ $$

This chic waterfront hotel at the edge of Fort Point Channel combines sophisticated architecture with luxurious decor of rich furnishings and textiles. Sumptuous bathrooms include a soaking tub as well as a walk-in shower.

Hotel Veritas
MAP C2 ▪ 1 Remington St, Cambridge, 02138 ▪ 617 520 5000 ▪ www. thehotelveritas.com ▪ $$

This luxury four-story boutique hotel located near Harvard is ideally sited for families visiting students. Combining luxury with convenience, rooms are intimate and contemporary, while bathrooms have marble finishes. A cozy lounge in the lobby serves cocktails.

Lenox Hotel
MAP L5 ▪ 61 Exeter St, 02116 ▪ 617 536 5300 ▪ www.lenoxhotel.com ▪ $$

Known for its exemplary service, luxurious modern comfort, historic elegance, and eco-innovation, this Back Bay boutique hotel near Copley Square has served Boston visitors since 1900. Many of the spacious corner rooms have wood-burning fireplaces. Dine at the City Table on New England seasonal fare, or at the Sólás authentic Irish Pub.

Loews Boston Hotel
MAP F5 ▪ 350 Stuart St, 02116 ▪ 617 266 7200 ▪ www.loewshotels.com/ boston-hotel ▪ $$

This posh boutique hotel in the handsome limestone former Boston police headquarters offers deluxe comfort and services in a convenient corner of South End.

W Hotel
MAP G5 ■ 100 Stuart St,
02116 ■ 617 261 8700
■ www.starwoodhotels.
com ■ $$
Seemingly designed as
much for the architectural
press as for the traveler,
this W appeals to visitors
who enjoy the convenient
location in the Theater
District at the edge of
Back Bay. A Bliss Spa
located in the hotel is
the ideal place to relax.

Hotel Commonwealth
MAP D5 ■ 500
Commonwealth Ave,
02215 ■ 617 933 5000
■ www.hotelcommon
wealth.com ■ $$$
Right by Kenmore Square,
this suave 245-room hotel
has all the high tech
essentials but with the
architecture and decor of
France's Second Empire.

Mid-Range Hotels

Courtyard Boston Cambridge
MAP B3 ■ 777 Memorial
Dr, Cambridge, 02139
■ 617 492 7777 ■ www.
marriott.com ■ $
Large desks and great
views are highlights of this
riverfront hotel. Amenities
include a fitness center
and a pool. The location
isn't ideal unless you have
a car to get around town.

Chandler Studios
MAP M6 ■ 54 Berkeley St,
02116 ■ 617 482 3450
■ www.chandlerstudios
boston.com ■ $$
This hip boutique hotel
in a South End brown-
stone offers studios with
ultra-modern furnishings,
kitchenettes, and high-
tech features. There's
a daily maid service
but no on-site staff.

The Charlesmark
MAP L5 ■ 655 Boylston
St, 02116 ■ 617 247 1212
■ www.charlesmarkhotel.
com ■ $$
Set in an 1892 Back Bay
townhouse, the compact
but ergonomic rooms of
this boutique hotel feature
custom-made furniture,
light-toned woodwork,
and smart Italian tilework.
Breakfast is included in
the astonishingly low
(for the area) rates.

Courtyard Boston Downtown
MAP N5 ■ 275 Tremont
St, 02116 ■ 617 426 1400
■ www.marriott.com ■ $$
Located at the edge of
the city's Theater District,
this 1920s tower hotel
underwent restoration
to give fresh glitter to its
dramatic public spaces
(think crystal chandeliers
and marble columns).
The rooms are small but
boast first-rate amenities.

Fairfield Inn & Suites Boston Cambridge
MAP F2 ■ 215 Monsignor
O'Brien Hwy, Cambridge,
02141 ■ 617 621 1999
■ www.fairfieldboston
cambridge.com ■ $$
This contemporary hotel
is just across the Charles
River from Downtown.
Rooms feature sleek
design including an ergo-
nomic workstation. There's
free Wi-Fi, free hot breakfast, and 24-hour fitness
and business centers.

Harborside Inn
MAP Q3 ■ 185 State St,
02109 ■ 617 723 7500
■ www.harborsideinn
boston.com ■ $$
This modest boutique
hotel is set in a historic
(1858) spice warehouse.
Rooms have wood floors,
exposed brick walls,
oriental rugs, and
traditional furnishings.

Inn at St Botolph
MAP E3 ■ 99 St Botolph
St, 02116 ■ 617 236 8099
■ www.innatstbotolph.
com ■ $$
Perfect for a romantic
getaway, this redbrick
townhouse boutique hotel
near Symphony Hall has
the finest in contemporary
design. The sunny rooms
have queen-size beds.

Kendall Hotel
MAP E3 ■ 350 Main St,
Cambridge, 02142
■ 617 577 1300 ■ www.
kendallhotel.com ■ $$
An artist-architect couple
transformed this century-
old Cambridge firehouse
into a boutique hotel. The
77 rooms are decorated
with an Americana folk
art theme. Don't miss
the Rooftop Retreat.

Sheraton Commander
MAP B1 ■ 16 Garden St,
Cambridge, 02138 ■ 617
547 4800 ■ www.sheraton
commander.com ■ $$
Harvard Square's original
(1927) hotel has elegant
contemporary decor.
Some rooms are small,
but public areas are
pleasantly clubby, and
the Cambridge Common
location is enchanting.

Westin Boston Waterfront
MAP P4 ■ 425 Summer
St, 02210 ■ 617 532 4600
■ www.starwoodhotels.
com ■ $$
Connected to the Boston
Convention and Exhibition
Center, this huge property
serves business travelers
well. Rooms offer great
city views.

Bed-and-Breakfast

Bowers House

9 Bowers Ave, Somerville, 02144 ▪ 617 680 6828 ▪ www.bowershousebnb. com ▪ $

The rooms in this friendly B&B are modern and individually decorated. The house is located in the hip Davis Square and is just a short subway ride away from all the main sights in the city.

A Friendly Inn at Harvard

MAP C1 ▪ 1673 Cambridge St, 02138 ▪ 617 547 7851 ▪ www.afinow.com ▪ $

This Queen Anne-style house is just steps from Harvard Square and the museums. The great location, gracious hospitality, and all mod cons, including internet access, make this a very popular hotel, particularly with visiting scholars and prospective students.

Clarendon Square Inn

MAP F6 ▪ 198 W Brookline St, 02118 ▪ 617 536 2229 ▪ www.clarendonsquare. com ▪ $

Comfortable, spacious, and sophisticated guest rooms and luxury suites are housed in a six-story South End Boston townhouse built in 1860. They offer designer fabrics, private bathrooms in limestone and marble, and the latest technology. There is no elevator.

Isaac Harding House

MAP C2 ▪ 288 Harvard St, Cambridge 02139 ▪ 617 876 2888 ▪ www.harding-house.com ▪ $

Set in a quiet Cambridge neighborhood, this remodeled 1860s

Victorian home is now a popular B&B. The 14 guest rooms are spacious and bright. Book direct for free parking.

Oasis Guest House

22 Edgerly Rd, 02115 ▪ 617 267 2262 ▪ www. oasisgh.com ▪ $

Close to Berklee School of Music, the Hynes Convention Center, and Symphony Hall, Oasis offers rooms in a townhouse located on a quiet one-way street a little removed from the hub-bub of Massachusetts Avenue. Guests can make use of a small, shared outdoor deck.

14 Union Park

MAP F6 ▪ 14 Union Park, 02118 ▪ 617 236 6961 ▪ www.14unionpark.com ▪ $$

Set on the most famous street in the South End, this 19th-century townhouse has been carefully restored with attractive, period detailing. The modern rooms are all elegantly furnished and feature stone en-suite bathrooms, walk-in closets, and Nespresso coffee makers.

Aisling Bed & Breakfast

MAP F6 ▪ 21 E Concord St, 02118 ▪ 617 206 8049 ▪ www.aisling-bostonbb. com ▪ $$

Housed in a 19th-century redbrick rowhouse on a tree-lined street in Boston's South End, this Victorian-style home features two comfortable en-suite guest rooms, central air conditioning, and free Wi-Fi. The two rooms have access to a shared kitchen.

Bertram Inn

92 Sewall Ave, Brookline, 02446 ▪ 617 566 2234 ▪ www.bertraminn.com ▪ $$

Set in a quiet residential neighborhood, this B&B began life as a private, Tudor-Revival-style home. Its rooms and small suites are all tastefully decorated with styles varying between Arts & Crafts, late Victorian, and just downright eclectic.

Irving House

MAP C1 ▪ 24 Irving St, Cambridge, 02138 ▪ 617 547 4600 ▪ www. irvinghouse.com ▪ $$

An older rooming house turned B&B, Irving House is tucked away in a leafy neighborhood next to Harvard. Rooms vary from tiny to spacious and some share bathrooms.

Moroccan Luxury Suites

MAP Q1 ▪ 8 Salem St, Charlestown, 02129 ▪ 617 953 4853 ▪ www. morrocanluxurysuites. com ▪ $$

This gorgeous Moroccan-themed B&B, housed in an 18th-century townhouse, features warm, comfortable rooms and suites with plush colorful furnishings, and a lovely garden courtyard.

Newbury Guest House

MAP K5 ▪ 261 Newbury St, 02116 ▪ 617 670 6000 ▪ www.newburyguest house.com ▪ $$

Several Back Bay homes have been linked to create this 32-room guesthouse. Rooms vary in size, but tend to be cozy with eclectic furnishings. Good value for the location.

Budget Hotels, Inns, and Hostels

Boston Common Hotel

MAP F5 ▪ 40 Trinity Pl, 02116 ▪ 617 933 7700 ▪ www.bostoncommon hotel.com ▪ $

One of the best-kept secrets of Back Bay, this once-private club offers cozy but comfortable rooms at relatively bargain rates. Some single rooms are available, and there are good discounts in low season.

DoubleTree Club

Columbia Point, Dorchester ▪ 240 Mt Vernon St, 02125 ▪ 617 822 3600 ▪ www.double tree3.hilton.com ▪ $

This recently renovated hotel is located near the HarborWalk and the John F. Kennedy Library and Museum. There's a free shuttle to the airport and local restaurants.

Hampton Inn

191 Monsignor O'Brien Hwy, Cambridge, 02141 ▪ 617 494 5300 ▪ www. hamptoninn3.hilton.com ▪ $

This chain hotel features high-speed internet in all rooms as well as free underground parking. Rooms are modest but include a good-sized desk area, making it popular with business travelers on a limited budget.

Holiday Inn Express

MAP F2 ▪ 250 Monsignor O'Brien Hwy, Cambridge, 02141 ▪ 617 577 7600 ▪ www.hiecambridge. com ▪ $

All of the rooms in this roadside motel have good work areas, microwaves, and refrigerators. There's limited free parking and it's only a short walk to the Lechmere "T" stop.

Hostelling International

MAP P5 ▪ 19 Stuart St, 02116 ▪ 617 536 9455 ▪ www.bostonhostel.org ▪ $

Set downtown, a short walk from popular sights, this modern hostel offers single-sex dorms with bunk beds, or private en-suite rooms with TV. Continental breakfast is included, and a communal kitchen and laundry rooms are available.

La Quinta Inn and Suites

23 Cummings St, Somerville, 02145 ▪ 617 625 5300 ▪ www.lq.com ▪ $

This motel is a short walk from the MBTA Orange Line and offers an airport shuttle service. Spacious rooms and suites have tasteful decor and offer cable TV and internet.

Chandler Inn

MAP M6 ▪ 26 Chandler St, 02116 ▪ 617 482 3450 ▪ www.chandlerinn.com ▪ $$

A popular choice for business travelers on a budget, this hotel in the South End is a short walk from Back Bay "T." All the rooms are comfortable, with TVs and phones.

College Club

MAP L4 ▪ 44 Commonwealth Ave, 02116 ▪ 617 536 9510 ▪ www.thecollegeclub ofboston.com ▪ $$

This private club, which is devoted to the promotion of higher education, also has guest rooms available in its sophisticated Back Bay townhouse. Several smaller rooms share bathrooms: these are only suitable for solo travelers.

Constitution Inn

MAP G2 ▪ 150 3rd Ave, Charlestown Navy Yard, Charlestown, 02129 ▪ 617 241 8400 ▪ www. constitutioninn.org ▪ $$

This 147-room facility in Charlestown Navy Yard serves military personnel, but welcomes all. Rooms are clean and modern, and guests can use the fitness center with pool and sauna free of charge.

Inn at Longwood Medical Center

342 Longwood Ave, 02115 ▪ 617 731 4700 ▪ www. innatlongwood.com ▪ $$

This is an attractive, comfortable 144-room hotel in the Longwood Medical Area. Families of patients get the best rates but it is open to all travelers.

Hotel 140

MAP F5 ▪ 140 Clarendon St, 02116 ▪ 617 585 5600 ▪ www.hotel140.com ▪ $$

Just around the corner from the Back Bay Amtrak station, this budget hotel has refurbished the rooms of the country's first YMCA into neat examples of how best to use small spaces.

Freepoint Hotel

220 Alewife Brook Pkwy, Cambridge, 02138 ▪ 617 491 8000 ▪ www.free pointhotel.com ▪ $$

Situated near the Alewife "T" station on the edge of Cambridge, Freepoint boasts chic style that suggests luxury, but with budget prices.

For a key to hotel price categories see p146

General Index

Page numbers in **bold** refer to main entries

A

Accommodation 145–51
Adams, John 22, 28
Adams, Samuel 44
  Boston Tea Party 14
  grave 12, 100, 101
  Paul Revere's ride 14
African-American community
  Black Heritage Trail 70, 82, 83
  George Middleton House 83
  Museum of African American History 81, 83
Air travel 138, 139
Alcohol 145
Alcott, Louisa May 45, 74
Ambulances 141
American football 73
American Revolution **14**, 42
Antiques shops 84
Aquarium, New England 7, 11, **38–9**, 52, 95, 97
Architecture
  Harvard University's "Architectural zoo" **23**
Arnold Arboretum 131
Art galleries
  Back Bay 90
  see also Museums and galleries
Artists' Open Studios 68
Asian restaurants 112
Attucks, Crispus
  grave 101

B

Back Bay 6, 25, **86–93**
  art galleries 90
  maps 86–7, 89
  nightclubs and bars 92
  restaurants 93
  shopping 91
  walk 89
Back Bay Fens 117
Bakeries, Italian 98
Ball, Thomas 18
Banks 140–41
  opening hours 142
Bars 60–61
  Back Bay 92
  Beacon Hill 85
  Cambridge and Somerville 128

Bars (cont.)
  Chinatown, the Theater District, and South End 111
  Downtown and the Financial District 104
  Kenmore and the Fenway 120
  North End and the Waterfront 99
  South of Boston 134
Baseball 73, 117
Basketball 73
The Beach
  day trips 76–7
Beach Street 107
Beaches
  Constitution Beach 46
  day trips 76–7
Beacon Hill 6, **80–85**
  antiques and gift shops 84
  maps 80, 83
  restaurants and bars 85
  walk 83
Beacon Street 82
Bed-and-Breakfast 150
Beer 61
Bell, Alexander Graham 43
La Berceuse (Van Gogh) 31
234 Berkeley Street 24
Berklee Performance Center 55, 89
Bernstein, Leonard 22
Bhutto, Benazir 22
Bicycles 139, 143
The Big Dig 43
Bindo Altoviti (Cellini) 34
Black Heritage Trail 70, 82, 83
Blaxton, William 19, 42
Boats
  boat tours 143
  Boston Duck Tours 52
  Boston Tea Party Ships and Museum 7, 96
  Charlestown Navy Yard **36–7**, 70, 95
  getting to Boston 138
  Head of the Charles Regatta 73
  paddle the Charles River 51
  Swan Boats 19, 52
  water taxis and ferries 139
Boch Center – Wang Theater 6, 54, 107
Bookstores 69
Boston Architectural College 25
Boston Calling 72

Boston Center for the Arts 54, 107, 109
Boston Common and Public Garden 6, 10, **18–19**, 71, 82
Boston Duck Tours 52
Boston Flower and Garden Show 72
Boston Harbor islands 48–9
Boston HarborWalk 71
Boston Marathon 43, 73
Boston Massacre (1770) 14
Boston Opera House 55
Boston Public Library 6, 42, 87, 89
Boston Tea Party (1773) 14
Boston Tea Party Ships and Museum 7, 96
Boston University 118
Boston's Center for Jewish Culture 83
Botticelli, Sandro 11, 34, 35
Bradstreet, Anne 45
Breweries 61
  Samuel Adams Brewery 51
Brighton Music Hall 57
Brooks, Rev. Phillips 32, 33
Budget travel 70–71
  hotels 151
Bulfinch, Charles 83
  Beacon Hill 44
  grave 101
  Harvard University 23
  Massachusetts State House 12, 15
  Nichols House Museum 81
  St. Stephen's Church 97
Bumpkin Island 48
Bunker Hill, Battle of (1775) 14
Bunker Hill Monument 36, 47
Burne-Jones, Edward 32
Busch-Reisinger Museum 21, 123
Buses 138

C

Cafés 66–7
Cambridge and Somerville 122–9
  maps 122–3, 125
  nightclubs and bars 128
  offbeat shops 126
  places to mix with the locals 127
  restaurants 129
  walk 125

Cambridge Arts River Festival 72–3
Cape Ann 76
Cape Cod 76
Captain Jackson's Historic Chocolate Shop 50
Cars 138–9, 141
Cassatt, Mary 30
Cassin Young, USS 36, 70
Castle, Wendell 31
Castle Island 46, 132
Cathedral, Holy Cross 109
see also Churches
Cellini, Benvenuto
Bindo Altoviti 34
Cemeteries
  Copp's Hill Burying Ground 13, 95, 97
  Forest Hills Cemetery 131
  ghosts and gravestones 51
  Mount Auburn Cemetery 70
  Old Granary Burying Ground 12, 101
Centre Street 132, 133
Cézanne, Paul 31
Charles Hayden Planetarium 17
Charles River 46
  Boston Duck Tours 52
  canoeing on 51
  Charles River banks 124
  Charles River Locks and Dam 47
  The Esplanade 87
  Head of the Charles Regatta 73
Charles Street 6, 69
Charlestown Bridge 47
Charlestown Navy Yard 7, **36–7**, 70, 95
Children 52–3
Children's Museum 52, 96
Chinatown, the Theater District, and South End 106–13
  Asian restaurants 112
  maps 106, 109
  nightclubs and bars 111
  restaurants 113
  shops 110
  walk 109
Chinese New Year 72
Christ in Majesty with Symbols 29
Christian Science Center 88–9
Christopher Columbus Park 47

Churches
  Church of the Covenant 24
  Emmanuel Church 24
  King's Chapel 12, 103
  Old North Church 13, 95, 97
  Park Street Church 12
  St. Stephen's Church 97
  Trinity Church 6, 11, **32–3**, 87, 89
  see also Cathedral
Civil War (1861–65) 42
Close, Chuck 31
Clubs *see* Nightclubs
Cole, Thomas 30
Columbus, Christopher statue of 47
Commonwealth Avenue 24, 88
Concord 74
Concord, Battle of (1775) 42
Constitution, USS 36, 37, 70
Constitution Beach 46
Coolidge, Charles 32
Copley, John Singleton 28, 30, 89
Copley Place 68
Copley Square 89
Copp, William 13
Copp's Hill Burying Ground 13, 95, 97
Credit cards 140–41
Crime 140
Crivelli, Carlo 35
Cummings, E. E. grave 131
Curley, James Michael 45
Currency 140–41
Custom House 102
Customs and immigration 140, 141
Cycling 139, 143

D
Dance and live music venues 56–7
Dance at Bougival (Renoir) 28
Dante Alighieri 34, 45
Davis Square 124
Day trips
  Historic New England 74–5
  The seaside 76–7
Declaration of Independence 12, 14
Deer Island 48
Degas, Edgar 31, 34
Dialing codes 141
Diller Scofidio + Renfro 96

Dine Out Boston 72
Disabled travelers *see* Travelers with specific needs
Discounts 71
Doctors 141
Dorchester Heights 14
Dorchester Heights Monument 47
Douglass, Frederick 81
Downtown and the Financial District 100–105
  bars and clubs 104
  maps 100, 101
  restaurants 105
  walk 103
Downtown Crossing 101
Driving 142
Du Bois, W. E. B. 22
Dudley Square 132–3
Dyer, Mary statue of 15

E
Eames, Charles 31
East India Company 14
Eddy, Mary Baker 44–5, 50
Edward M. Kennedy Institute for the United States Senate 133
Electrical appliances 142
Eliot, T. S. 22
Embassies 141
Emerald Necklace 19, 130, 131
Emergency services 140, 141
Emerson, Ralph Waldo 45, 74, 102
Emmanuel Church 24
Entertainment
  dance and live music venues 56–7
  gay and lesbian hang-outs 58–9
  performing arts venues 54–5
The Esplanade 46, 87
Estey, Alexander 24
Ether Monument 19
Events 72–3

F
Faneuil Hall 6, 13, 101
Faneuil Hall Marketplace 69
Feast of St. Anthony 73
Fenway *see* Kenmore and the Fenway
Fenway Park 7, 53, 117, 119
Ferries 139

Festivals and events 72–3
Financial District see Downtown and the Financial District
Fire services 141
First Night 73
Fish Pier 46
Fitzgerald, John "Honey Fitz" 45, 97
Fitzgerald, Rose 97
Fogg Museum 21, 123
Food and drink 144–5 see also Bars; Cafés; Restaurants
Forest Hills Cemetery 131
Fort Independence 71
Fort Point Channel 46
Foster, Norman 28, 30
Founders' Memorial 19
Fourth of July 73
Franklin, Benjamin 101
Franklin Park 131
Franklin Park Zoo 53
Free events 70–71
Freedom Trail 6, 7, 10, **12–13**, 43, 70, 81
French, Daniel Chester 131
French Cultural Center 24
Frog Pond 53
Fuller, Buckminster grave 70

G

Galleries see Museums and galleries
Gallops Island 49
Gardens see Parks and gardens
Gardner, Isabella Stewart 35, 117
Garment District 68
Garrison, William Lloyd 81 statue of 88
Garrity, W. Arthur, Jr. 45
Gates, Bill 22
Gay and lesbian hangouts 58–9
George Middleton House 83
Georges Island 48
Ghosts and gravestones 51
Gibson House Museum 25, 88
Gift shops 84
Gillette, King Camp 43
Grape Island 48
El Greco 31
Greenway Carousel 53
Grocers, Italian 98
Gropius, Walter 23, 123
Guided tours 71

H

Hampton Beach 77
Hancock, John 14, 28
Handel, G. F. Messiah 32
Harrison Gray Otis House 82
Harry Widener Memorial Library 20
Harvard, John 20, 42 statue of 20, 125
Harvard Art Museums 21, 123, 125
The Harvard Lampoon 21
Harvard Square 7, 70 bookstores 69
Harvard University 7, 10, **20–23**, 42, 123 alumni **22** "Architectural zoo" **23**
Harvard Yard 125
Hatch Shell 54, 70
Hawthorne, Nathaniel 74
Head of the Charles Regatta 73
Health care 140, 141
History 42–5 American Revolution **14** day trips 74–5 Freedom Trail **12–13**
Hockey 73
Holy Cross Cathedral 109
Homer, Winslow 30
Hospitals 141
Hostels 151
Hotels 145–51 budget hotels 151 deluxe hotels 147–8 hip/historic stays 148–9 luxury hotels 146–7 mid-range hotels 149
Howard Gotlieb Archival Research Center 118, 119
Howe, Elias 43
Hyatt Boston Harbor 47
Hyatt Regency Cambridge 47

I

Ice hockey 73
Inman Square 124
Innovations 43
Inns 151
Institute of Contemporary Art 96
Insurance 140
Internet 142
Ipswich 77
Irish immigrants 42, 72

Isabella Stewart Gardner Museum 6, 8–9, 11, **34–5**, 117, 119
Islands Boston Harbor 48–9
Italian bakeries and grocers 98

J

Jamaica Pond 131, 133
James II, King 12
James, Henry 22, 45
La Japonaise (Monet) 29
Jews Boston's Center for Jewish Culture 83 New England Holocaust Memorial 50
John F. Kennedy Library and Museum 7, 133
John J. Moakley Courthouse Park 47
Jordan Hall 55, 118, 119

K

Kenmore and the Fenway 116–21 maps 116, 119 nightclubs and bars 120 restaurants 121
Kenmore Square 119
Kennedy, Edward M. 133
Kennedy, John F. 22, 42, 45, 97 John F. Kennedy Library and Museum 7, 133 statue of 15
Kennedy, Joseph 45
King's Chapel 12, 103

L

La Farge, John 11, 32, 33, 89
Ladder District 101
Land, Edwin 43
Lawn on D, The 51
Le Corbusier 23, 123
Lehane, Dennis 45
Lexington 74
Lexington, Battle of (1775) 14
Libraries Boston Public Library 6, 42, 87, 89 Harry Widener Memorial Library 20 John F. Kennedy Library and Museum 7, 133 Mary Baker Eddy Library 50
Lilac Sunday 72
Little Brewster Island 49
Loeb Drama Center 23, 124

Long Wharf 7, 46
Longfellow, Henry Wadsworth 14, 45
grave 70
Longfellow House 50, 124–5
Longfellow Bridge 47
Longfellow House 50, 124–5
Lost property 140
Lovells Island 48
Lowell 75
Lowell, Robert 45

M

McCloskey, Robert 18
McCormick, Elizabeth Day 30
McKay, Donald 44
McKim, Mead & White 87
Magazines 142
Maloof, Sam 31
Manet, Edouard 34
Mapparium 50, 89
Maps
  Back Bay 86–7, 89
  Beacon Hill 80, 83
  Boston 6–7
  Boston Harbor islands 49
  Boston highlights 10–11
  Cambridge and Somerville 122–3, 125
  children's activities 53
  Chinatown, the Theater District, and South End 106, 109
  dance and live music venues 56
  day trips: historic New England 75
  day trips: the seaside 77
  Downtown and the Financial District 100, 101
  Freedom Trail 12–13
  gay and lesbian hang-outs 59
  Harvard University 20–21
  Kenmore and the Fenway 116, 119
  North End and the Waterfront 94, 97
  off the beaten path 51
  performing arts venues 55
  restaurants 63
  shopping 69
  South of Boston 130, 133
  spots for seafood 64
Marathon 43, 73

Markets
  Boston Public Market 68
  Faneuil Hall 69, 101
  Quincy Market 13, 101, 103
  SoWa Open Market 69
Martha's Vineyard 77
Mary Baker Eddy Library 50
Mason, James 44
Massachusetts College of Art and Design Galleries 119
Massachusetts Institute of Technology (MIT) 125
Massachusetts State House 12, **15**, 81, 83
Mather, Increase 44
Matisse, Henri 34, 35
Middleton, George 83
Milmore, Martin 18
Minute Men 42
Mobile phones 141
Monet, Claude 31
  La Japonaise 29
Money 140–41
Money-saving tips 71
Monuments and memorials
  Bunker Hill Monument 36, 47
  Dorchester Heights Monument 47
  Ether Monument 19
  Founders' Memorial 19
  New England Holocaust Memorial 50
  Shaw Memorial 18, 42
  Soldiers and Sailors Moment 18
Mount Auburn Cemetery 70
Multicultural Arts Center 124
Museums and galleries
  money-saving tips 71
  opening hours 142
  Boston Center for the Arts 107
  Boston Tea Party Ships and Museum 7, 96
  Children's Museum 52, 96
  Gibson House Museum 25, 88
  Harvard Art Museums 21, 123, 125
  Howard Gotlieb Archival Research Center 118, 119
  Institute of Contemporary Art 96
  Isabella Stewart Gardner Museum 6, 8–9, 11, **34–5**, 117, 119

Museums and galleries (cont.)
  John F. Kennedy Library and Museum 7, 133
  Longfellow House 124–5
  Massachusetts College of Art and Design Galleries 119
  MIT Museum 125
  Museum of African American History 81, 83
  Museum of Fine Arts, Boston 6, 7, 11, **28–31**, 109, 117, 119
  Museum of Natural History 20, 123
  Museum of Science 6, 7, 10, **16–17**, 52, 125
  Nichols House Museum 81
  Old Sturbridge Village 75
  Paul Revere House 10, 13, 95, 97
  Paul S. Russell, MD Museum of Medical History and Innovation 51
  Peabody Museum 7, 21, 123
  Semitic Museum 21
  Sports Museum of New England 50
  USS Constitution Museum 37
  Warren Anatomical Museum 118
Music
  money-saving tips 71
  dance and live music venues 56–7
  performing arts venues 54–5

N

Nantucket Island 76–7
Natural History Museum 20, 123
New Bedford 74
New England
  day trips 74–5
New England Aquarium 7, 11, **38–9**, 52, 95, 97
New England Conservatory 55
New England Historic Genealogical Society 24
New England Holocaust Memorial 50
New Year 72, 73
Newbury Street 6, 7, 11, **24–5**, 68, 87
Newburyport 77
Newman, Robert 13, 95
Newport 75

Newspapers 142
Nichols, Rose 81
Nichols House Museum 81
Nightclubs
Back Bay 92
Cambridge and Somerville 128
Chinatown, the Theater District, and South End 111
Downtown and the Financial District 104
Kenmore and the Fenway 120
South of Boston 134
North End and the Waterfront 78–9, 94–9
Italian bakeries and grocers 98
maps 94, 97
restaurants and bars 99
walk 97
Northern Avenue Bridge 40–41

O
Obama, Barack 22
O'Brien, Conan 21
Old Corner Bookstore 102
Old Granary Burying Ground 12, 101
Old North Church 13, 95, 97
Old South Meeting House 12, 102
Old State House 12, 101
Old Sturbridge Village 75
Olmsted, Frederick Law
Emerald Necklace 19, 130, 131
Franklin Park 131
Jamaica Pond 131
World's End 49
O'Neill, Eugene
grave 131
Opening hours 142
Otis, Harrison Gray 44, 82

P
Paramino, John F. 19
Park Street Church 12
Parker, Robert 45
Parkman, George 19, 82
Parkman Bandstand 19
Parkman House 82
Parks and gardens
Arnold Arboretum 131
Back Bay Fens 117
Boston Common and Public Garden 6, 10, **18–19**, 82

Parks and gardens (cont.)
Boston Flower and Garden Show 72
Christopher Columbus Park 47
Emerald Necklace 130, 131
The Esplanade 87
Fenway Park 53
Franklin Park 131
Jamaica Pond 131, 133
John J. Moakley Courthouse Park 47
Puopolo Park 47, 97
Rose Kennedy Greenway 97
Rose Kennedy Rose Garden 97
Southwest Corridor Park 109
Union Park 108, 109
Passports 140, 141
Paul Revere House 10, 13, 95, 97
Paul S. Russell, MD Museum of Medical History and Innovation 51
Peabody Museum 7, 21, 123
Peddocks Island 48
Pei, I. M. 87, 89, 133
Performing arts venues 54–5
Personal security 140
Pharmacies 141
Piano, Renzo 21, 23, 34, 119, 123
Piano Row 108
Pinsky, Robert 45
Planetarium, Charles Hayden 17
Pleasure Bay 132
Plymouth 74
Police 140, 141
Pollock, Jackson 31
Portsmouth 75
Post Office Square 102–3
Postal services 142, 143
Providence 75
Prudential Center 88, 89
Prudential Skywalk 47, 53
Public transportation 138, 139
Puopolo Park 47, 97
Puritans 42, 44

Q
Quincy Market 13, 101, 103

R
Railways 138, 139
Raphael 11, 35
Rembrandt 11, 31, 34

Renoir, Pierre Auguste 31
Dance at Bougival 28
Restaurants 62–3, 144–5
Back Bay 93
Beacon Hill 85
Cambridge and Somerville 129
Chinatown, the Theater District, and South End 112–13
Downtown and the Financial District 105
Kenmore and the Fenway 121
North End and the Waterfront 99
South of Boston 135
spots for seafood 64–5
Revere, Paul 44
grave 100, 101
Old North Church 13, 95
Paul Revere House 10, 13, 95, 97
Paul Revere's ride 14, 42
St. Stephen's Church 97
silverwork 28
Revere Beach 77
Revolution *see* American Revolution
Richardson, Henry Hobson
Harvard University 23
Trinity Church 11, 32, 87
Trinity Church Rectory 25
Roosevelt, Franklin Delano 22
Rose Kennedy Greenway 97
Rose Kennedy Rose Garden 97
Rowe, Jonathan 15
Rowes Wharf 47
Rubens, Peter Paul 31
Russell, Paul S. 51
Rye Beach 77

S
Sabine, Walter Clement 117
Sackler Museum 21, 123
Safety 140, 141
Saint-Gaudens, Augustus
Shaw Memorial 18
St. Patrick's Day 72
St. Stephen's Church 97
Salem 74
Samuel Adams Brewery 51

Sanders Theatre 6, 55
Sargent, John Singer
    Boston Public Library
    87, 89
    Isabella Stewart Gardner
    Museum 34
    Museum of Fine Arts,
    Boston 28, 30
    *Portrait of Isabella Stewart
    Gardner* 35
Science, Museum of 6, 7,
    10, **16–17**, 52, 125
Scofield, William 43
Seafood 64–5
Semitic Museum 21
Sert, Josep Lluís 23
Shakespeare on Boston
    Common 71
Shaw, Robert 18
Shaw Memorial 18, 42
Ships *see* Boats
Shopping 68–9, 144–5
    antiques and gift shops
    84
    Back Bay 91
    Cambridge and
    Somerville 126
    Chinatown, the Theater
    District, and South End
    110
    Italian bakeries and
    grocers 98
    opening hours 142
Soccer 73
Soldiers and Sailors
    Monument 18
Somerville *see* Cambridge
    and Somerville
Somerville Theatre 54,
    124
Sons of Liberty 14
South of Boston 130–35
    bars and clubs 134
    maps 130, 133
    restaurants 135
    walk 133
South End *see* Chinatown,
    the Theater District, and
    South End
South Station 108
Southwest Corridor
    Park 109
SoWa Open Market
    69
Spectacle Island 48
Spirit of Boston Cruises
    47
Sports 73
Sports Museum of New
    England 50

Stebbins, Hugh 23
Stirling, James 23
Stuart, Gilbert 30
Subway 42, 138
Swan Boats 19, 52
Symphony Hall 6, 54,
    117

T
Taxis 139
TD Garden 55
Telephones 142
Theater
    Boch Center – Wang
    Theater 6, 54, 107
    money-saving tips 71
    Sanders Theatre 6, 55
    Shakespeare on Boston
    Common 71
    Somerville Theatre 54,
    124
Theater District *see*
    Chinatown, the Theater
    District, and South End
Thomas, General John
    133
Thompson Island 49
Thoreau, Henry David 74,
    102
Time zone 142
Titian 31, 34
Tomlinson, Ray 43
Tourist information 142,
    143
Trains 138, 139
Travel 138–9
    money-saving tips 71
Travel insurance 140
Travel safety advice 140,
    141
Travelers with specific
    needs 140–41
Tremont Street 42, 107
Trinity Church 6, 11, **32–3**,
    87, 89
Trinity Church Rectory
    25
Trips and tours 143
Trolley buses 138, 143
Tubman, Harriet 109

U
Union Park 108, 109
Universities
    Boston University
    118
    Harvard University 7,
    10, **20–23**, 42, 123
Upham's Corner 132
Upjohn, Richard 24

V
Vaccinations 140
Van Gogh, Vincent
    La Berceuse 31
Vermeer, Jan 34
Veronese, Paolo 35
Views 47
Villa Victoria 108
Visas 140, 141
Visitor information 142,
    143

W
Walks 139, 143
    Back Bay 89
    Beacon Hill 83
    Cambridge and
    Somerville 125
    Chinatown, the Theater
    District, and South End
    109
    Downtown and the
    Financial District 103
    Kenmore and the Fenway
    119
    North End and the
    Waterfront 97
    South of Boston 133
Warren, Dr. John Collins
    118
Warren Anatomical
    Museum 118
Washington, George 20
    American Revolution 14
    bust of 97
    statue of 10, 18, 82
    Washington's
    Headquarters 50, 124–5
Water taxis 139
Waterfront 46–7
    see also North End and
    the Waterfront
Weather 142
Webster, Daniel
    statue of 15
Webster, Dr. John 82
Weeks Footbridge 47
West, Dorothy 45
Whale-watching 143
Whitney, Anne 88
William III, King 44
Winthrop, John 42, 44
    Founders' Memorial 19
    grave 12, 100, 101
World's End 49
Writers 45

Z
Zoo, Franklin Park 53
Zuckerberg, Mark 43

Acknowledgments

Author

Patricia Harris and David Lyon write about travel, food, fine arts, and popular culture for many publications including *Boston Magazine*, *Boston Globe*, *Yankee*, *Robb Report*, and hungrytravelers. com. They also co-wrote the Dorling Kindersley *Eyewitness Travel Guide* to Boston.

Jonathan Schultz is a travel writer based in Portland, Maine. He has contributed extensive local content to *Boston Magazine*, Boston. citysearch.com; LosAngeles.citysearch.com; as well as having compiled a guide to Boston for Z Publishing.

Additional contributors
Paul Franklin, Nancy Mikula

Publishing Director Georgina Dee

Publisher Vivien Antwi

Design Director Phil Ormerod

Editorial Michelle Crane, Rebecca Flynn, Rachel Fox, Fay Franklin, Hayley Maher, Freddie Marriage, Fíodhna Ní Ghríofa, Scarlett O'Hara, Sally Schafer, Ankita Sharma, Neil Simpson

Cover Design Maxine Pedliham, Vinita Venugopal

Design Marisa Renzullo

Picture Research Susie Peachey, Ellen Root, Lucy Sienkowska, Oran Tarjan

Cartography Subhashree Bharti, Suresh Kumar, James Macdonald, Simonetta Giori, Dominic Beddow

DTP Jason Little, George Nimmo

Production Linda Dare

Factchecker Pat Harris & David Lyon

Proofreader Kathryn Glendenning

Indexer Hilary Bird

Illustrator Lee Redmond

First edition created by Departure Lounge, London

Revisions Sophie Adam, Parnika Bagla, Marc Di Duca, Alice Fewery, Sumita Khatwani, Shikha Kulkarni, Maresa Manara, Alison McGill, Bhavika Mathur, Bandana Paul, Azeem Siddiqui, Rachel Thompson, Ankita Awasthi Tröger

Commissioned Photography John Coletti, Demetrio Carrasco, Rough Guides/Angus Osborn, Rough Guides/Susannah Sayler, Tony Souter, Linda Whitwam.

Picture Credits

The publisher would like to thank the following for their kind permission to reproduce their photographs:
Key: a-above; b-below/bottom; c-centre; f-far; l-left; r-right; t-top

Alamy Images: Hank Abernathy 101tl; Marcus Baker 72tl; Alastair Balderstone 75cla; M. Scott Brauer 74crb; David Coleman 133clb; Stephen Coyne 7tr; Shay Culligan 106cl; Richard Cummins 69tr; Ian Dagnall 56br; Ian G Dagnall 57tl, 95tr; Randy Duchaine 51cr; Eagle Visions Photography / Craig Lovell 122tr; Raymond Forbes 103cla; Jeff Greenberg 6 of 6 /*The Thinker, Frogs of Tadpole*

Playground (2003) by David Phillips The City of Boston, The Boston Art Commission 53cr; Della Huff 4cra, 4crb, 98ca; Andre Jenny 37tl; JLImages 18bc; Kim Karpeles 53tr; Melvyn Longhurst 100tl; LOOK/Elan Fleisher 83tl, 99cl; Mary Evans Picture Library 42tl; Terry Mathews 25crb; Paul Matzner 116cra; Megapress 52br; Debra Millet 104btl; Steven Milne 13crb; NATUREWOLRD 47cla; Niday Picture Library /*Portrait of Samuel Adams* (1772) by John Singleton Copley 44clb; Nikreates 24cla, 42cb; Stuart Pearce 11cr, 98bl; North Wind Picture Archives 43tr; Anthony Pleva 130c; Prisma Bildagentur AG/Heeb Christian 111tl; Valery Rizzo 61tl; Rosalrene Betancourt 7 18cla; Science History Images 14t; Sherab 92b; Lee Snider 80cla; Superstock/George Ostertag 36–7.

Aquitaine: 113tr.

Barbara Lynch Gruppo: 67tl, 69clb, 111br. **Beacon Hill Bistro:** 85cr. **Beacon Hill Chocolates:** 84cb. **Berklee College of Music:** 55tr. **Bostonian Society:** 12ca. **Boston Playwrights Theatre:** Kalman Zabarsky 118cl. **Boston Symphony Orchestra:** Marco Borggreve 54t; Stu Rosner 117tr. **Courtesy of the Museum of Science, Boston:** Michael Malyszko 16cra, 17tr. **Museum of Fine Arts, Boston:** 11cra, 28c, 28clb, 29tl, 29crb, 30ca, 30bl, 31tl, 31cr; *Mr and Mrs Isaac Winsow* (1773) by John Singleton Copley 28br; *Lullaby: Madame Augustine Roulin Rocking a Cradle (La Berceuse)* (1889) by Vincent van Gogh 31bl. **Bridgeman Images:** AA World Travel Library 33tr; Houston 45tr.

Multicultural Arts Centre: Yi-Lin Hung Photography 124clb. **Children's Museum, Boston:** Paul Specht 52tl, 96tl. **Club Cafe:** 58tl. **Corbis:** Bettmann 22tl; Massimo Borchi 2tl, 8–9; National Geographic Creative/Brian J. Skerry 52b; Richard T. Nowitz 10cra; Andria Patino / *Boston Women Memorial* (2003) by Meredith Gang Bergman The City of Boston, The Boston Art Commission 88–9.

Courtesy of the artist and Barbara Krakow Gallery: work by Jackie Ferrara at "Surface: Summer Group Show", June 8, 2013 – July 26, 2013. 90bl.

Courtesy of the Nichols House Museum, Boston, MA: Gilded bronze bust of wreathed Victory (1902) by Augustus Saint-Gaudens 80tr.

David Lyon & Patricia Harris: 90c, 104br. **Devonia Antiques:** 84tl. **Dreamstime.com:** Americanspirit 95bl; Anastassiyal 127tl; Berniephillips 11br; Jon Bilous 12br, 46bl, 81t, 96b; Joaquin Ossorio Castillo 77cla; Angel Claudio 49t; Jerry Coli 16crb; David931 19bl; Dejavu Designs 48br; Songquan Deng 86tl; Kristy Durbridge 36bc, 52tl; Joachim Eckel 22cb; Elena Elisseeva 3tl, 78–9; F11photo 13c, 47tr, 102t, 107t; Ritu Jethani 102cb, 131br; Wangkun Jia 94tr; Mary Lane 101br; Chee-onn Leong 4b, 11clb, 32bl, 76t; Wei Chuan Liu 73tr; Luckydoor 6cla; Lunamarina 2tr, 3tr, 6–7t, 40–41, 136–7; Giuseppe Di Paolo 4clb; Sean Pavone 1, 4t, 18–19, 114–15; Peanutroaster 52c; Thomas Price 46tl; Rcavalleri 26–7; Jorge Salcedo 88b, 119bl; Marcio Silva 10bl, 20cla, 24–5c, 69tr, 103bl, 108b, 123cr; Peter Spirer 125cl; Vvoevale 112cla; Wenling01 68tl; Tsz Wai Wong 12cl; Jixue Yang 24bc, 56cl.

Fairmont Copley Plaza: Richard Mandelkorn 60b.
Fogg Art Museum: President and Fellows of
Harvard College/Natalja Kent 21tc. **Freedom
Trail Foundation:** 52cb.

Tres Gatos: 135cl. **Getty Images:** Boston Globe
50crb, 54crb, 57tl, 69br, 71bl, 75tr, 97cla, 111ca,
112br, 124tr; 126crb, /Ed Farrand 45cl; Kevork
Djansezian 43clb; Steve Dunwell 118t, 132t;
Education Images 82b; Lou Jones 57crb, 107bc;
Lonely Planet 10cl; Maremagnum 87tr; Cindy Ord
61br; S. Greg Panosian 10crb; Greg Pease 58cl;
Joe Robbins 117b; Stock Montage 44tc; Denis Jr.
Tangney 43tl. **Greater Boston Convention &
Visitors Bureau:** Boston Harbor Association 53cl.
Grill 23: 93br.

Harvard Museum of Natural History: 20cb.
Harvest: 67crb.

Isabella Stewart Gardner Museum: 34cl, 34bl;
The Ascension of Christ (15th century) Russian,
Novogorod, Tempera on panel, 52 x 36 cm (20 1/2
x 14 3/16 in.) 11cb; Sienna Scarff 34–5; *Portrait of
Isabella Stewart Gardner* (1888) by John Singer
Sargent 35tl.

L.A. Burdick Chocolatiers: 71tr. **L'Espalier
Restaurant:** 62cl. **Legal Sea Foods:** Gustav Hoiland
105tr; Heath Robbins 68cb. **Lekker Home:** 110tr.
David Lyon: 120tr.

Magpie: Danielle Freiman 126ca. **The Middle
East:** 128tl.

New England Aquarium: 38crb, 38bl, 38–9, 39tl.
Newbury Comics: 91cl.

**Peabody Museum of Archaeology & Ethnology
Harvard University:** President and Fellows of
Harvard College 21bl.

Robert Harding Picture Library: Franz Marc Frei
4cr; James Kirkikis 4cla; Michael Neelon 36cla.

Sweet Cheeks Q: 121clb. **Tadpole:** 110bl. **The
Hawthorne:** Gustav Hoiland 120bl. **The Kirkland
Tap & Trotter:** Michael Piazza 129clb. **The Sports
Museum:** 50tl. **The Thinking Cup:** Bill Lyons 70t.
UNI: 62cb. **USS Constitution Museum:** 37ca.

Cover

Front and Spine: **Dreamstime.com.**
Sean Pavone.

Back: **Alamy Stock Photo:** Stan Tess tl;
Dreamstime.com: Chee-onn Leong cla, Sean
Pavone bc, Sean Pavone crb, Marcio Silva tr.

Pull Out Map Cover

Dreamstime.com: Sean Pavone.

All other images © Dorling Kindersley

For further information see: www.dkimages.com

*As a guide to abbreviations in visitor information
blocks:* ***Adm*** *= admission charge;* ***D*** *= dinner;*
L *= lunch.*

MIX
Paper from
responsible sources
FSC™ C018179
www.fsc.org

Penguin
Random
House

Printed and bound in China

First edition 2003

Published in Great Britain by
Dorling Kindersley Limited
80 Strand, London WC2R 0RL

Published in the United States by
DK US, 1450 Broadway, Suite 801,
New York, NY 10018, USA

Copyright © 2003, 2019 Dorling
Kindersley Limited

A Penguin Random House Company

19 20 21 22 10 9 8 7 6 5 4 3 2 1

**Reprinted with revisions 2005, 2007, 2009,
2011, 2013, 2015, 2016, 2018, 2019**

A CIP catalog record is available
from the British Library.

A catalog record for this book is available
from the Library of Congress.

ISSN 1479-344X
ISBN 978-0-2413-6478-9

Street Index

Acorn Street	N3	Dalton Street	K6	Keany Square	P1	Portland Street	P1
Albany Street	G6	Dartmouth Street	L4	Kenmore Square	D5	Prescott Street	B2
Anderson Bridge	B2	Davis Square	C1	Kilmarnock Street	D5	Prince Street	Q1
Anderson Street	N2	Dedham Street	F6	Kingston Street	P4	Prospect Street	D1
Appian Way	B1	Devonshire Street	Q4	Kirkland Street	C1	Purchase Street	Q4
Arch Street	Q4	Divinity Avenue	C1	Kneeland Street	P5	Queensbury Street	D6
Arlington Street	M4	Dorchester Avenue	Q5	Lansdowne Street	D5	Quincy Street	B1
Atlantic Avenue	R3	Dunster Street	B2	Leverett Circle	N1	Revere Street	N3
Avenue de Lafayette	P4	East Berkeley Street	G5	Lincoln Street	P5	Richmond Street	Q2
Avenue Louis		East Newton Street	F6	Longfellow Bridge	M2	River Street	M3
Pasteur	D6	Eliot Bridge	A2	Louisburg Square	N3	River Street	
Avery Street	P4	Eliot Square	B1	Main Street	D3	(Cambridge)	C3
Back Street	D5	Eliot Street	N5	Margin Street	Q1	River Street Bridge	B3
Batterymarch Street	Q3	Embankment Road	M3	Marginal Road	N6	Riverway	C6
Bay State Road	D5	Endicott Street	Q1	Marlborough Street	L4	Rutherford Avenue	F1
Beach Street	P5	Essex Street	Q5	Mason Street	P4	Rutland Street	F6
Beacon Street	L4	Evelyn Moakley		Mason Street		Saint James Avenue	M5
Beacon Street		Bridge	R4	(Cambridge)	B1	Salem Street	Q1
(Cambridge)	C1	Everett Street	B1	Massachusetts		School Street	P3
Belvidere Street	K6	Exchange Place	Q3	Avenue	J5	Shawmut Avenue	N6
Berkeley Street	M4	Exeter Street	K5	Merrimac Street	P2	Sleeper Street	R5
Blackstone Street	Q2	Fairfield Street	K5	Milk Street	Q3	Soldiers Field Road	A2
Blossom Street	N1	Federal Street	Q4	Monsignor McGrath		Somerset Street	P3
Boston University		Fenway	D6	Highway	E1	Somerville Avenue	D1
Bridge	C4	Fleet Street	R1	Monsignor Reynolds		South Charles Street	N5
Bowdoin Street	P3	Franklin Street	Q4	Way	F6	South Street	Q5
Boylston Street	L5	Fruit Street	M2	Monument Square	G1	Springfield Street	F6
Brattle Street	B1	Fulton Street	Q2	Moon Street	R1	Staniford Street	P2
Broad Street	Q3	Gainsborough Street	E6	Mount Vernon		State Street	Q3
Broadway	D2	Garden Court	Q1	Street	N3	Story Street	B1
Bromfield Street	P3	Garden Street	N2	Myrtle Street	N3	Stuart Street	N5
Brookline Avenue	C6	Garden Street		Nashua Street	N1	Summer Street	P4
Cambridge Parkway	F2	(Cambridge)	B1	New Chardon Street	P2	Summer Street	
Cambridge Street	B3	Gloucester Street	K5	New Rutherford		Bridge	R5
Cambridge Street		Grove Street	N2	Avenue	G2	Symphony Road	E6
(Cambridge)	C1	Hampshire Street	D2	New Sudbury Street	P2	Temple Street	P2
Canal Street	P1	Hancock Street	N2	Newbury Street	L5	Thatcher Street	Q1
Cardinal O'Connell		Hanover Avenue	R1	North Bennett		Tileston Street	Q1
Way	N2	Hanover Street	Q2	Street	Q1	Tremont Street	N6
Causeway Street	P1	Harris Street	R1	North Square	Q2	Union Park Street	F6
Charles River Dam	F2	Harrison Avenue	P5	North Street	R2	Union Street	Q2
Charles Street	N4	Harvard Bridge	J4	North Washington		Unity Street	Q1
Charlesgate	D5	Harvard Square	B1	Street	Q1	Van Ness Street	D5
Charlestown Avenue	F2	Harvard Street	C2	Northampton Street	E6	Walnut Street	N3
Charlestown Bridge	G2	Haymarket Square	P2	Northern Avenue	R4	Warenton Street	N5
Charter Street	Q1	Hemenway Street	J6	Northern Avenue		Warren Avenue	F5
Chatham Street	Q3	Herald Street	N6	Bridge	R4	Warren Street	G1
Chauncy Street	P4	Hereford Street	J5	Old Northern		Washington Street	P5
Chestnut Street	N3	High Street	Q4	Avenue	R4	Washington Street	
Church Street	N5	Hilliard Street	B1	Oliver Street	Q3	(Cambridge)	C1
Clarendon Street	L4	Holyoke Street	B2	Otis Street	Q4	Waterhouse Street	B1
Clark Street	R1	Hudson Street	P5	Otis Street		Webster Avenue	D1
Clearway Street	K6	Hull Street	Q1	(Cambridge)	E2	West 4th Street	G6
Clinton Street	Q2	Huntington Avenue	K6	Oxford Street	B1	West Brookline	
Columbus Avenue	M6	India Street	Q3	Park Drive	D5	Street	F6
Commercial Avenue	F3	Inman Square	D1	Park Plaza	M5	West Canton Street	F6
Commercial Street	R1	Ipswich Street	D5	Park Street	P3	West Cedar Street	M3
Commonwealth		Irving Street	N2	Peabody Street	B1	West Newton Street	F5
Avenue	J5	James J. Storrow		Pearl Street	Q4	Western Avenue	B3
Concord Street	F6	Memorial Drive	K4	Pembroke Street	F6	Western Avenue	
Congress Street	Q4	Jersey Street	D5	Peterborough Street	D5	Bridge	B3
Congress Street		John F. Kennedy		Phillips Street	N2	Westland Avenue	E5
Bridge	R5	Street	B2	Piano Row	N4	Winter Street	P4
Cooper Street	Q1	John W. Weeks		Pilgrim Road	C6	Worcester Street	F6
Court Street	Q3	Footbridge	B2	Pinckney Street	N3	Worthington Street	D6
Cross Street	Q2	Joy Street	N3	Plynpton Street	B1	Yawkey Way	D5